T0287654

CELEBRATING COVENTRY

WILL ADAMS

AMBERLEY

First published 2020

Amberley Publishing, The Hill, Stroud
Gloucestershire GL5 4EP

www.amberley-books.com

Copyright © Will Adams, 2020

Unless otherwise credited, all the photographs were taken by the author during the autumn and
winter of 2019.

British Library Cataloguing in Publication Data.
A catalogue record for this book is available from the British Library.

ISBN 978 1 4456 9816 8 (print)
ISBN 978 1 4456 9817 5 (ebook)

Typesetting by Aura Technology and Software Services, India.
Printed in Great Britain.

Contents

Introduction – Coventry Fact and Fiction

Mention Coventry and most people will know of the wartime Blitz and the new cathedral. They may think of the car industry, and envisage modern shopping in pedestrianised areas, and modern glass and concrete tower blocks.

But cities are like great forests. As each season passes, so the 'old growth' is subsumed beneath the new 'shoots', like so much architectural leaf-mould. The layers build up century upon century until ancient buildings and street patterns are lost or transformed beyond recognition. This process was, of course, hastened in Coventry by the Blitz of 14/15 November 1940, a kind of appalling forest fire that obliterated two-thirds of the city centre. However, a surprising amount of Coventry's ancient history survives amid and beneath the modern city. The purpose of this book is to dig down and sort through the layers to provide a sketch of a city of many facets, of deep-rooted history and lively legends.

What of the name itself? The *Oxford Dictionary of Place-names* defines it as probably 'Cofa's tree' – a boundary marker for lands held by a Saxon landowner, Cofa, about whom nothing is known. Or is it from the earlier spelling 'Couaentree', a farmed village ('trev') near the River Cune or Couen, an ancient name for the Sherbourne? Or 'Convent town', from St Osburga's monastic house?

The city arms might also be a source of surprise, at its centre being an elephant – an animal not generally associated with the midlands of England. The shield is spilt in two – red for Coventry and green for Lichfield, representing the joint diocese. The elephant represents power – the power to carry a three-towered castle on its back – although no one would have seen such a living beast in the fourteenth century. The wild cat above is a symbol of watchfulness. In early versions the elephant stands in front of an oak tree – that of Cofa? The motto, 'Camera Principis' – Chamber or Court of the Prince – is said to derive from Edward the Black Prince, who held Cheylesmore Manor. But the arms were conferred by his father, Edward III, at the incorporation of the city in 1345, and the 'Principis' may simply refer to the city's many royal connections. In 1959 supporters were granted the black eagle of Earl Leofric on the left and the phoenix on the right, symbolising the resurgence of the city after the wartime destruction.

Above: The city coat of arms as it appears above the main entrance to the Council House.

Right: The elephant and castle have been perched high above the Upper Precinct since the post-war redevelopment, probably unseen by most.

Most people will be familiar with the phrase 'to be sent to Coventry', meaning to refuse to associate or speak to someone. Some say this arises from when Royalist prisoners were kept in the city during the Civil War, and were shunned by the citizens of this Parliamentary stronghold.

Another phrase associated with the city is 'as true as Coventry blue'. In its weaving and dyeing days, Coventry was famous for a blue thread that was guaranteed not to fade.

At Christmastime we sing the 'Coventry carol' – 'Lully, lullay, thou little tiny child' – which dates from the sixteenth century, when part of the Coventry Mystery Plays depicted the birth of Christ. It is a lullaby for children doomed to be slain by Herod.

Another local religious connection is the 'Coventry godcake', a triangular mince tart traditionally given to godchildren by their godparents at New Year as a symbol of good luck. Local people still refer to the triangular traffic island at a T-junction as a 'godcake'.

Finally, there is a legend that St George was born and died in Coventry, the only place in England to make such a claim. But as with much of the folklore of this fascinating city – who knows?

This is by necessity very much a 'whistle-stop' tour, and though its purpose is to celebrate Coventry, it can only scratch the surface of a city with a thousand years of history. Many readers will be yelling in exasperation that so much has had to be left out – but using this book as your starting point, please dig further. It will be well worth the effort.

I have consulted a good many books and websites for the information, which I hope is accurate, but any errors are mine alone.

Pre-war Architectural Heritage

I knew it was an old place, but I was surprised to find how much of the past, in soaring stone and carved wood, still remained in the city.

J. B. Priestley

The Three Spires

On the morning of 15 November 1940 Coventry was a wasteland of smouldering rubble, but standing defiantly above the destruction were the city's famous 'three spires' – St Michael's, Holy Trinity and Christ Church. Although now rather eclipsed by today's soaring architecture, the three spires could once be viewed from afar and were a symbol of the city for centuries.

St Michael's Church – the 'old cathedral' – was the city's parish church from 1249, and one of the largest in England, with a spire that, at 295 feet (90 metres) high, is only surpassed by Salisbury and Norwich. It began life in the twelfth century as the chapel of the city's castle (St Michael's in the bailey), and was then extensively rebuilt from the early fifteenth century. As well as a double aisle to the north, there were also side chapels dedicated to the city's prosperous medieval guilds. By the end of the nineteenth century the building was in need of repair, and major restoration work was undertaken in 1885–90.

Coventry's first cathedral, St Mary's, dated from the beginning of the twelfth century, and had been a joint see with Lichfield. It was the only cathedral church in England to be completely demolished at the Reformation, and the city had to wait some 400 years until 1918 for St Michael's to become the cathedral of the resurrected diocese.

Then just after 7.00 p.m. on the night of 14 November 1940 the great air attack on Coventry commenced. Incendiary bombs landed on the cathedral, some lodging between the leaded roof and the nave vaulting. Despite the valiant efforts of firefighters, the water supply failed and the fire raged out of control. Many of the church's valuables were removed, and the only tomb to survive was that of the new diocese's first bishop, H. W. Yeatman-Biggs; his effigy holds a small model of the cathedral.

Above left: St Michael's Church is seen in all its pre-war, pre-cathedral glory in this old postcard. (Author's collection)

Above right: Today the tower and spire still soar skywards, miraculously having survived the Blitz.

Below: The interior of the cathedral before it was destroyed by incendiary bombs.

Above: Towering above the empty shell of the old cathedral is the linked porch of the new.

Right: A cross of charred beams stands in front of the inscription 'Father Forgive' behind the altar.

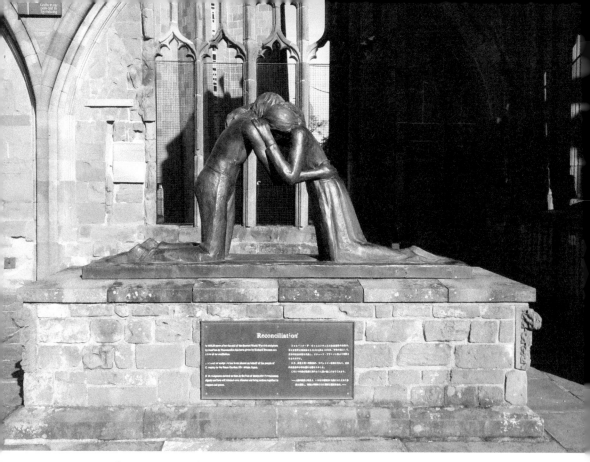

Reconciliation is central to the ministry of Coventry Cathedral, and this sculpture, by Josefina de Vasconcellos, stands in the ruins. Originally called *Reunion*, in 1995 (to mark the fifty years since the end of the war) bronze casts, renamed *Reconciliation*, were placed here and in the Hiroshima Peace Park in Japan.

Steel girders fixed in the roof during the 1880s restoration were distorted by the heat, and brought down the roof pillars and clerestory walls into the nave, leaving only the external walls and the spire largely intact. On the morning of the 15th a local vicar picked up three large medieval nails from the roof, tied them into a cross with wire and placed them on an altar of rubble; later the cathedral's stonemason, Jock Forbes, fashioned a cross from charred oak roof beams. This cross, a replica of which stands behind altar today, instantly became the focal point of the ruins, together with the words 'Father Forgive' inscribed in the wall behind it.

Only a short distance from St Michael's is the second of the three spires, that of Holy Trinity, the city's other medieval parish church. Like St Michael's, it was first mentioned in the early twelfth century. Medieval rebuilding made it one of the longest parish churches in England, at 194 feet (59 metres). Its spire stands 237 feet (72 metres) high, replacing one that collapsed into the church in 1666. Unlike the old cathedral, it is cruciform in shape, with a central tower and spire. A notable feature is a 1430s painting of the Last Judgement, known as the 'Coventry Doom'; after years of painstaking restoration, this remarkable medieval discovery was revealed in all its glory in 2004.

Holy Trinity was much restored externally from the late eighteenth to the beginning of the twentieth century, but its remarkable survival during the Blitz makes it, according to architectural historian Nikolaus Pevsner, 'an especially important monument to the medieval prosperity and cultural richness of the city, a fine building handsomely decorated and furnished'.

The third spire fared less well even than St Michael's. Christ Church, located between New Union Street and Warwick Lane, has a quite different history. Greyfriars friary was established by Franciscan monks in 1234, and in around 1350 a fine steeple, 230 feet (70 metres) high, was added. The friary disappeared following the Dissolution of the Monasteries in the 1530s, and ownership passed to the city; in 1830–32, as the city grew, a new church was added to the steeple, which was now at one end rather than in the middle. This survived the 1940 Blitz, but was hit during a subsequent raid in 1941. The ruins were demolished in 1950, leaving the tower and spire in isolation for the second time in the church's history, and a new Christ Church was built in Cheylesmore in 1954–57 to replace it.

Below left: The great length and cruciform shape of Holy Trinity are clearly seen in this view from the old cathedral tower.

Below right: Christchurch, the third of the city's 'three spires', stands alone since the demolition of the remainder of the building. The rather incongruous modern architecture of The Wave, an 'indoor waterpark', stands next door.

Religious Houses

Mention has already been made of first cathedral, St Mary's. This was the church of a Benedictine priory, established in 1043 by Leofric, Earl of Mercia, and his wife Godiva, on the site of an earlier nunnery founded by St Osburga, which had been destroyed by Danes under King Cnut in 1016. Generously endowed, it became a monastery and cathedral in 1102. The building was cruciform in shape, and may have had three spires like Lichfield Cathedral.

At the Dissolution, Henry VIII offered the cathedral buildings to the city, but the necessary money could not be raised, so the king had the buildings demolished, and the stonework was plundered. However, one tower survived and was used as a house until 1714. Subsequently the Blue Coat School was established on the site, and during building work in the 1850s some remains were discovered. Excavations in the 1960s revealed more, and in the 1990s Channel 4's *Time Team* made further discoveries, returning in 2001 for further explorations, the results now easily appreciated by the visitor.

Another religious house that has fared rather better is Whitefriars, at the beginning of what is now the London Road, in the shadow of one of the ring road flyovers. It was founded as a Carmelite settlement in 1342, and here was once

Below and opposite above: The 'muscular Gothic sandstone' (Pevsner) of the Blue Coat School, built on the remains of the north-west tower of the ancient St Mary's Cathedral, was unfortunately enshrouded in scaffolding at the time of my visit, and can be better appreciated from the accompanying Victorian engraving. On the left are the pretty Lychgate Cottages, restored in the mid-nineteenth century.

Below: The Priory Garden with pedestrian walkways gives an idea of the huge scale of the original cathedral, which was 425 feet long, much longer than St Michael's. An associated visitor centre contains some archaeological finds.

another church, which excavations proved to have been very large; it was used as a school for a short time, but at the Dissolution much of it was demolished. However, the two-storey eastern range of the cloisters in red sandstone was saved when purchased by Oxford scholar John Hales as his residence, Hales Place. Hales was one of the King's Commissioners appointed to dissolve the Coventry monasteries. He also bought the old Hospital of St John in the city in 1545, of which more later. Medieval stalls and misericords from Whitefriars were transferred to the school, where they remain to this day.

There is a particularly fine sixteenth-century oriel window on the upper floor; tradition has it that Elizabeth I addressed the crowds from here during a visit to Coventry in 1565 as a guest of Hales. In 1569–70 Mary Queen of Scots was held in the city on Elizabeth's orders, and spent part of that time at Whitefriars. Damaged during the war, the building became a Salvation Army hostel in 1948, then after restoration in 1965 it became a museum, which has since closed. It is currently owned by the Herbert Art Gallery & Museum. The friary's gatehouse survives in Much Park Street.

Another surviving gatehouse is that of the former Cheylesmore Manor (pronounced 'Chiles-more'), which can be found hidden away behind an office block on New Union Street. The manor originated with Leofric and Godiva, and was later the home to the Earls of Chester. Later Queen Isabella and her grandson Edward the Black Prince were owners, and Edward's son, Richard II, had the city walls diverted to include the manor; it is said to have been the only unfortified royal residence outside London. It remained Crown property until 1819, when it was sold to the lessee, the Marquis of Hertford. Thereafter the land was gradually built over.

A historical re-enactment in front of Whitefriars, date unknown: 'James I and Princess Elizabeth, and City Guards'. (Author's collection)

From the central oriel window, Elizabeth I is traditionally said to have addressed the crowds during a visit to the city in 1565. Today this fine building is rather hemmed in by the ring road.

The manor survived the Second World War, having been converted into flats, but despite its historical pedigree it was demolished in the mid-1950s. However, the gatehouse and two cross-wings remain, and they were restored in 1966–68. Since then the building has housed the city's register office (making it the oldest in Britain), with sympathetic modern additions.

In 1385 Richard II and Queen Anne laid the foundation stone for the Charterhouse, or St Anne's Priory, a short distance from the city beside the River Sherbourne on what is now London Road. An internationally important Grade I listed Carthusian monastery, it was the sixth of only nine ever built in Britain, and was completed in the early fifteenth century. As with other religious houses in Coventry it suffered at the Dissolution of the Monasteries, when the chapel and other buildings were destroyed and used as building materials. Happily, much of the original priory buildings survived, albeit altered internally. A remarkable feature is the only remaining Carthusian wall painting in the UK, discovered in the late nineteenth century hidden behind panelling. Originally 23 feet wide by 13 feet high (7 by 4 metres), only the lower part remains.

The Charterhouse was used as a private home from 1848 until 1940, when it was given to the city by the owner, Sir William Wyley, as a centre for arts and culture. Today the whole site is a Scheduled Ancient Monument, but has been placed on the Heritage at Risk register due to problems with the roof. In 2012 it passed to what is now the charity Historic Coventry Trust, which is restoring it and the adjoining parkland.

Above: The surviving gatehouse of Cheylesmore Manor is hidden away behind an office block on New Union Street, and now houses the city's register office.

Left: The Elizabethan timber-framed north end of the Charterhouse. Having fallen into considerable disrepair, the whole building is undergoing thorough restoration by the Historic Coventry Trust, thanks to a Heritage Lottery Grant of £4.3 million.

St John the Baptist Church was established when Edward II's widow, Queen Isabella, gave land at 'Babbelak' to the medieval Guild of St John the Baptist in 1344, to build a chapel for prayer. Following Henry VIII's dissolution of the guilds, the church closed in the 1540s. A century later, during the Civil War, it was used as a prison for captured Scottish Royalist soldiers, who inflicted much damage. The building was later used as stables, a market and a dyeing house for cloth until, in 1734, though ruinous, it became a parish church once more.

The church was restored in 1858–61 and again in 1875–77 by the celebrated Gothic architect Sir George Gilbert Scott, who added the battlemented parapets and exterior buttresses, and a pulpit and reredos in medieval style. A brass plate records the height of the water that flooded the church to a depth of 5 feet on 31 December 1900, when the River Sherbourne (now mostly culverted beneath the city centre) burst its banks. As a result of the great damage done, the church was forced to close for seven weeks. Originally built on piles on the site of a lake, during the 1870s restorations the parish council had wanted Scott to raise the church by some 4 feet, but he had said that such expenditure was unnecessary, as the chances of flooding were minimal!

The church boasts a fine east window, and below it an 1879 alabaster reredos depicting the Ascension, originally richly coloured and gilded and claimed to have been copied from a Giotto painting.

St John's survived the Blitz, but was damaged by fire in 1945.

Built mostly in the fifteenth century, St John's suffered mixed fortunes until becoming a parish church again in 1734. It was much restored by Sir George Gilbert Scott in the nineteenth century.

Civic Buildings

Dating from the same time as Whitefriars, St Mary's Guildhall, in Bayley Lane, hard against the south wall of the old cathedral, was begun in 1340–42 for the merchant guild of St Mary (the guilds were fraternities for the city's leading businessmen, and regulated trade). It is, according to Pevsner, 'one of the most notable surviving medieval guildhalls in Britain'. Occupying what had been the edge of the old castle yard, building continued until the mid-fifteenth century, and it eventually housed four guilds, which merged to become the powerful and influential Trinity Guild. It was also used as the council house; the city's first mayor, John Ward, was created there in 1349 (a tradition that lasted until 2002, when greater space was needed). It also served as a theatre, and it is almost certain that William Shakespeare would have appeared here. After the guilds were dissolved in 1552, the hall passed to the city corporation. Restoration took place in the 1820s/'30s, and in the 1941 Blitz the roof was damaged by incendiary bombs, and Caesar's Tower, then the city's oldest standing structure, was almost totally destroyed, although treasures stored in its basement for safe-keeping largely survived. The hall's rare Flemish 'Coventry Tapestry', dating from around 1500 and measuring 9 by 3 metres, was stored at Keresley Colliery. Post-war restoration was completed in 1952–53, and in 1956 the hall was linked by an internal bridge to the 'new' Council House behind.

The classic view of the north end of St Mary's Hall, facing Bayley Lane. Beneath the window inside hangs the famous late fifteenth-century 'Coventry Tapestry'.

The Guildhall is built around a courtyard, and the early fifteenth-century hall is 76 feet long by 30 feet wide (23.2 by 9.1 metres), built above a vaulted crypt and a kitchen with massive fireplaces. It boasts a grand window overlooking Bayley Lane, a splendid panelled roof with colourful angel bosses, and a minstrels' gallery. Today it continues in its role as the primary venue for prestigious civic functions.

Moving forward to the eighteenth century, in Cuckoo Lane is the former County Hall, opened in 1783 and one of the city's few public buildings to survive from that era. It stands on the highest point in the city centre, possibly the site of the twelfth-century castle, and was used as the county court – Coventry was both a city and a 30-square-mile county from 1451 until 1842, when it rejoined the county of Warwickshire. The Prison Governor's house was attached, facing Pepper Lane. The prison itself was demolished in 1867 to make way for a new city library. Perhaps the most notable trial was that of Mary Ball in 1849, who had poisoned her abusive husband. Found guilty, she was hanged outside the building – the last public execution in the city – in front of a crowd of 20,000 spectators.

The building was bought from the county by the city in 1936, and after the Crown Court moved to Much Park Street in 1988 the building lay empty until the ground floor was converted into a bar in 2000; it is now part of a pub group. Although the interior has been redesigned, the judge's chair and public gallery have been left in situ, and the old prison cells are used as dining areas.

The first-floor Doric portico and pediment of County Hall of 1784 on Cuckoo Lane. It is now occupied by a Slug & Lettuce pub.

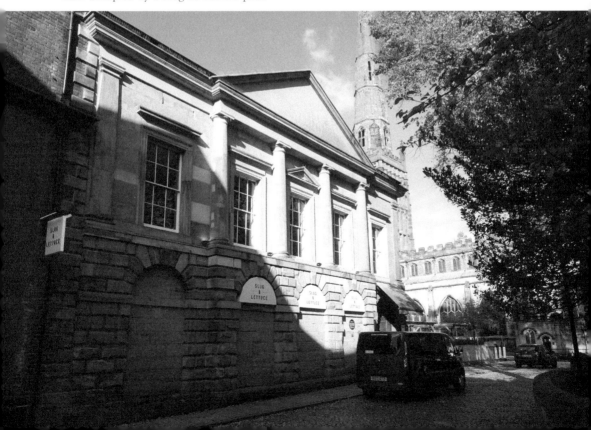

Nearby in Bayley Lane is the Drapers' Hall, built in 1831–32 in the Greek Revival style. A kind of architectural 'time capsule', it boasts decorative plaster ceilings, Victorian kitchens, and a ballroom with orchestra balcony and mirrored walls. Unusually, being surrounded by other buildings it was originally constructed without windows and was entirely top-lit; windows were added later, spoiling the symmetry of the Corinthian columned façade.

Sadly this exceptional Grade II*listed Regency building, a wartime survivor, stood empty and redundant for many years, but is now to be restored and reopened, hopefully in time for Coventry's role as UK City of Culture in 2021. It is intended that it will be a classical music and education venue, and a performance and rehearsal space for the university's School of Performing Arts. It will also become a base for the Drapers' Guild – its original owners – who will return some of the original furniture.

Of the many twentieth-century pre-war buildings in the city, the Council House in Earl Street is worthy of mention. St Mary's Guildhall had become too small for its purpose, and many departments had been moved to other locations around the city. A new, larger council house was needed. Many years in the planning,

Drapers' Hall in Bayley Lane stood next to the site of The Drapery, the largest medieval cloth market outside London, cloth having been an important source of medieval Coventry's wealth. The Council House can be glimpsed to the right, the new Herbert Art Gallery to the left.

The Council House is a striking building, although Pevsner considers that, for a building opened in 1920, it 'reflects the medieval past rather than the city's emerging industrial future'.

the new building was the result of a 1910 competition. It was built in 1913–16, and officially opened in 1920 by the future King George VI, who would visit the windowless, bombed-out building again in 1940, following the Blitz. It is in the Tudor Revival style, with a tower at the St Mary's Street corner, from which projects a clock. The ornamented façade features statuary, including Leofric, Godiva and the figure of Justice. An early suggestion was for shops along the ground floor, but this was discarded.

The City Walls

Back in 1329 Edward III had given permission for taxes to be collected to finance walls to protect what was already a wealthy city with considerable commercial and strategic importance. The extended and expensive construction began in the mid-1350s and lasted for more than forty years, and it was not until the 1530s that the walls took their final completed form – having absorbed a great deal of money along the way! Just over 2 miles (3.5 km) long and consisting of two sandstone walls with a rubble and mortar infill, the walls were at least 8 feet (2.4 metres) thick and more than 12 feet (3.7 metres) high. King Richard II contributed by allowing stone to be quarried from his park at Cheylesmore.

A well-preserved section of the city wall runs through what is now Lady Herbert's Garden, between Swanswell Gate and Cook Street Gate.

John Speed's 1610 map of Coventry shows twelve gates and twenty towers. The city was described as one of the best defended in England, although the wall was more symbolic than defensive. It did, however, enable Parliamentarian Coventry to refuse entry to Charles I during the Civil War. It is thought that Coventry's opposition to the Royalist cause may have been a reason why the newly restored Charles II ordered the walls to be demolished in 1662, leaving only the gates standing. In around three weeks the work of decades was in ruins, although remains survived till the late eighteenth century.

By that time the gates had all been removed save two – Swanswell Gate and Cook Street Gate. The latter was presented to the city in 1913 by local benefactor Sir William Wyley, founder of Coventry's Chamber of Commerce and twice mayor in 1911–13. The similar Swanswell Gate was also known as Priory Gate, having been a private entrance for St Mary's Priory, which required the wall to be diverted to include the priory fishponds – today's Pool Meadow area. Its archway was blocked in the 1850s and it became a dwelling, but was presented to the city by Sir Alfred Herbert in 1932, who also financed the preservation of the surviving wall.

Above left: The fifteenth-century Cook Street Gate, seen here from within the walls, was restored in 1918.

Above right: Swanswell Gate, also seen from within the walls, became a residence in the 1850s, the arch blocked.

Ford's and Bond's Hospitals

Moving forward to the sixteenth century, Ford's Hospital is a set of half-timbered almshouses in Greyfriars Lane ('hospital' in this sense comes from the Latin word for 'hospitable', and signified a kind of early charitable sheltered housing). It was endowed by William Ford, a wool merchant and former mayor, upon his death in 1509 to provide accommodation for six elderly people – five men and one woman. Within twenty years the hospital had been extended twice to accommodate more people, including couples; after 1800 it catered for women only, and by the middle of that century was said to accommodate forty.

During the Blitz a single bomb hit the building, killing the warden, a nurse and six residents; in 1951–53 the severely damaged building was restored using original materials where possible. Today the modernised almshouses provide comfortable flatlets for seven women.

Also currently managed by Coventry Church Municipal Charities is Bond's Hospital in Hill Street, and like Ford's it offers a high standard of private, self-contained apartments for people of limited means from all walks of life, with resident staff. Back in 1344 Queen Isabella gave land known as 'Babbelak' to the

Above: Pevsner considers the 'profusely decorated' Ford's Hospital, restored in 1953 following Blitz damage, to be 'perhaps the finest of Coventry's surviving timber-framed buildings'.

Left: The hospital's narrow courtyard, seen here in an old postcard, is considered a particularly fine example of English domestic architecture of the period. (Author's collection)

The courtyard of Bond's Hospital has on the north side a range of buildings restored in the 1830s, while the original sixteenth-century buildings are on the right, also heavily restored.

Guild of St John to build a church, the original St John the Baptist Church, already mentioned above. Supporting the church was a college of priests, and by 1364 a 'Bablake school' is recorded.

The will of Thomas Bond, a wealthy draper and another former mayor of Coventry, who died in 1506, endowed the hospital, attached to the school, for ten poor men together with a woman to 'dress their meat'. The two institutions shared a courtyard, and the same people often served as governors of both. There was also a strong connection between school and church; in 1734 the vicar of St John's was also the headmaster. The present buildings date from around 1560. The school expanded during the nineteenth century after several sizeable bequests, and in the 1890s moved to its present site in Coundon Road.

Although much restored in the early nineteenth century, the Grade II* listed hospital still retains most of its original features; the gabled tiled roof has carved bargeboards, and there are diamond lattice casement windows and massive ashlar chimneys. In the early 1970s the small hospital rooms were converted into bedsits, and ten new flats were added in 1985. Another addition was Bond's Court, also in Hill Street, comprising twenty-seven self-contained apartments, opened in 1985 by Diana, Princess of Wales. The garden contains a section of the old city wall.

The Coventry Cross

An important city landmark was the Coventry Cross, which stood at the junction of Cross Cheaping and the old Broadgate ('cheaping' being an Old English word for 'market', as in Chipping Norton, etc.). Replacing earlier versions, a new cross was begun in 1541, financed by £200 left in the will of Coventry-born Mayor of London Sir William Holles. Completed in 1544, the cross was brightly painted, but deteriorated over the years until 1771, when it was dismantled to avoid collapse. A statue of King Henry VI was saved and is now in the Herbert Art Gallery & Museum.

In the 1930s a replica was proposed, but it was not until the 1970s that the plan came to fruition. A new cross, 57 feet (17.4 metres) high by George Wagstaff, was erected in 1976 next to Holy Trinity Church, around 100 metres from its original site. Unlike the original it was mainly made from cast red ferro-concrete, with some carved stone statues; twenty niches contained the figures of kings, saints and monks, animals and angels. Unfortunately in recent years the cross has been removed by the City Council to make way for a larger outdoor seating area for Cathedral Lanes, and currently future plans for it are unknown.

The Golden Cross was much rebuilt in the nineteenth century, so it is difficult to know which parts are original. It was further sympathetically refurbished in 2016–17.

Nearby, in Hay Lane, the three-storey timber-framed and jettied Golden Cross pub, probably named after the cross, is claimed to be the oldest pub in Coventry (and one of the oldest in the Midlands). The building is said to date from 1583, and has been a pub since 1661.

Spon Street Townscape Scheme

The city end of Spon Street has been a Conservation Area since 1969 and now provides an excellent opportunity to view some of the city's medieval architecture gathered in one place. The area includes St John's Church, Bond's Hospital and the old Bablake School, and it is hoped to extend it to include the old 'top shops' (early nineteenth-century well-lit upper-storey domestic workshops) in Lower Holyhead Road, and buildings in Hill Street.

Spon Street was originally part of an important east–west route through the city from Gosford Street, with a gate in the city walls. Formerly occupied by

Well-lit 'top shops' above houses at the bottom of Holyhead Road, from the early nineteenth century. The wall in the right background is where the ring road severed the city end of Telford's road.

13-29
LOWER HOLYHEAD ROAD
BUILT 1819-1837. THE SURVIVING PART OF A LONG RANGE OF 18 HOUSES WITH WORKSHOPS ON THE UPPER FLOORS, KNOWN AS 'TOPSHOPS'. WITH LARGE WINDOWS. USED BY CRAFTSMEN IN THE WEAVING AND WATCHMAKING TRADES BEFORE THE ADVENT OF STEAM POWERED FACTORIES. RESTORED TO RESIDENTIAL USE IN 1984 BY COVENTRY CHURCHES HOUSING ASSOCIATION.

many different trades, by the nineteenth century cloth and leather production
(located near the edge of the city because of the noxious smells and substances
employed) had given way to watchmaking. (The Coventry Watch Museum
is housed in one of the preserved buildings.) Increasingly built-up, the street
escaped major wartime destruction, but afterwards fell into neglect and disrepair,
and some surviving medieval houses were demolished and replaced by modern
flats. However, the 1960s brought a greater awareness of the city's disappearing
medieval architectural heritage, and it was decided to preserve the best of the
remaining buildings between St John's Church and the new ring road (which had
severed the street), and to move others and re-erect them here as part of the Spon
Street Townscape Scheme. The first transplanted building arrived in 1969–70;
subsequently some twelve buildings were restored in situ, and ten have been
re-erected from elsewhere, most statutorily listed, so 'Medieval Spon Street' now
boasts some of the best medieval timber-framed buildings in the country and is
a 'living museum' of Coventry's vernacular architectural heritage as well as an
attractive environment for specialised shopping.

Some of the in-situ and transplanted buildings in 'Historic Spon Street'. The tall
three-storey building was a typical merchant's house and once stood in Much Park Street
before being moved here and re-erected in the early 1970s.

The Coventry Watch Museum occupies Nos 22, 23 and 24 in Court 7 in Spon Street. The premises are probably the last example of what was a common dwelling arrangement in the eighteenth and nineteenth centuries, and house a huge display of clocks and watches, many Coventry-made. (Courtesy of Coventry Watch Museum)

Post-war Regeneration

> The multi-level shopping centre at Coventry, with its trees and banks of flowers, its sheltered walks and pleasant relationship of buildings is, by consensus, one of the finest built anywhere.
>
> Lewis Mumford, *The City in History* (1961)

The splendid largely medieval city, with its many timber buildings and narrow streets, tall spires and fine municipal buildings – think present-day York or Canterbury – stood until the fateful night of 14 November 1940, and the subsequent raids in 1941 and 1942. Such was the level of destruction that Nazi Minister of Propaganda Joseph Goebbels coined the term *coventriert* ('coventried') when describing similar devastating raids. Some 500 tons of high explosives were dropped in wave after wave of attacks, essentially flattening the city centre.

This gave the planners a 'clean sheet' to work with, and immediately after the war a reconstruction committee headed by William (later 1st Baron) Rootes was set up. What emerged was the so-called 'Gibson Plan', formulated by twenty-nine-year-old Manchester-born town planner Donald Gibson, and already under consideration in 1938 to ease congestion in the cramped medieval city centre. The resultant 'pedestrianisation' – the separation of motor traffic and pedestrians – was a completely new town planning concept. Coventry's 'Precinct', Upper (1951–56) and Lower (1957–60), was the first of its kind in Europe. Central Government supported the scheme as a template for further developments elsewhere.

Another Coventry first was the UK's first street drinking ban – an alcohol-free zone – put into place in the city centre in 1988, and subsequently adopted elsewhere.

Broadgate and the Precinct

Broadgate was one of the first reconstruction projects. The original narrow street, widened in Victorian times, was replaced by a square at the head of the Precinct, opened by Princess Elizabeth, the future Queen, in May 1948. In the centre was

Sir William Reid Dick's bronze statue of Lady Godiva, unveiled in October 1949, and there were gifts of bulbs and shrubs from the people of the Netherlands. Beyond, and completing the rising vista from the Precinct, was the focal point of the old cathedral tower and spire.

The surrounding buildings began with Broadgate House of 1948–53, and the Owen Owen department store and Hotel Leofric in 1955; the latter was claimed to be the country's first post-war city hotel built with British finance. On the east side, cutting across the view of the cathedral, a row of 'temporary' shops with corrugated fronts was built; these became a city landmark in their own right, surviving until March 1974!

On the south side of Broadgate is a popular mechanical clock. Every hour, when the bell strikes, the figure of Lady Godiva riding a white horse emerges from one door and leaves through another, while above her another window opens to reveal 'Peeping Tom', who takes a quick peep then covers his eyes and withdraws, supposedly struck blind. The clock and bell, dating from 1870, came from the city's old Market Hall, whose tower survived the bombing but was unsafe. The mechanism and tracks were made by local college apprentices, while Lady Godiva, her horse and Peeping Tom were carved from wood by sculptor Trevor Tennant.

A notable feature of the city's redevelopment was the circular Market Hall, now Grade II listed. It is 276 feet (84 metres) in diameter and contains 160 island stalls with a further forty 'shop stalls' set into the perimeter wall. Built in 1957 and opened the following year by Princess Alexandra, it was claimed to

This wonderful between-the-wars photograph of Broadgate shows the bustling heart of the city, complete with trams. It is interesting to speculate how modern traffic would cope with it if it had survived the war – pedestrianised, no doubt! (Author's collection)

COVENTRY . BROADGATE.

Above: Early post-war development is seen here, with the new Broadgate island in situ and planted out, and the 'temporary' post-war shops on the right, not removed until 1974. Holy Trinity church dominates the view. (Author's collection)

Below: Now the Owen Owen department store and Leofric Hotel of 1953–54 have been built on the north side. (Author's collection)

Above: Broadgate was pedestrianised and lost its 'island status' in 2012. Poor Lady Godiva, rotated through 90 degrees, is now lost amongst whatever the new open space can accommodate, in this case a fairground – previously the island was strictly out of bounds!

Below: Looking back to the south side of the new Broadgate, we see Broadgate House, the first of Donald Gibson's new city centre buildings (1948–53), spanning Hertford Street.

BROADGATE HOUSE. COVENTRY.

BROADGATE HOUSE

The first major building to set the pattern of redevelopment in the replanned centre was erected by the City Council and declared open by the Rt-Hon-Lord Silkin, formerly Minister of Town & Country Planning, on 2 May 1953

Members of the Redevelopment Committee—

Chairman	Councillor E·M·Rogers
Vice-Chairman	Alderman G·E·Hodgkinson OBE
The Mayor	Alderman B·H·Gardner
Deputy Mayor	Alderman H·B·W·Cresswell
	Alderman J·Fennell
	Alderman A·R·Grindlay CBE·JP
	Alderman V·A·Hammond
	Councillor D·M·Balsillie
	Councillor W·A·Binks
	Councillor J·Daniels
	Councillor E·McGarry
	Councillor T·Meffen
	Councillor C·Melbourne
	Councillor E·A·C·Roberts
	Councillor G·W·Sheridan
	Councillor C·D·Swain
	Councillor F·Walsh

Charles Barratt	Town Clerk
A·H·Marshall	City Treasurer
Donald Gibson CBE City Architect & Planning Officer	
Victor Hill	City Estate Surveyor
Consulting Engineers	Scott & Wilson
General Contractors	Higgs & Hill Ltd.

Above: Since 1953 the Godiva Clock in Broadgate has entertained residents and visitors when, on the hour, Godiva rides around the balcony spied on by boggle-eyed Peeping Tom!

Left: This plaque beneath Broadgate House survives to pay credit to those involved in the post-war rebuilding.

be the first large-scale post-war covered market in England. It was given a flat roof to accommodate a car park, and the ramp up to it was originally heated to prevent icing!

The upper storey of the Precinct proved an unsatisfactory idea, as shoppers were reluctant to climb stairs to visit the shops; this was rectified by the provision of a rather obtrusive escalator, which was to be removed in 2019. A City Council spokesman said, 'The Upper Precinct is going to feel much more open and modern once the escalator is out of the way and then we can crack on with the bigger work which will see new paving, planting, trees and water features installed.' Perhaps something of the original concept is to be restored, although decades of redevelopment have grafted onto the original vision many new buildings in succeeding architectural styles, a mishmash that has effectively destroyed the original vistas, and the clean – albeit perhaps rather austere and 1950s 'right-angular' – lines of the Precinct. In addition, Broadgate itself has subsequently been pedestrianised, the Godiva statue moved and realigned, and the Cathedral Lanes shopping centre of 1986/90 blocking the view towards the cathedral.

Today a range of other redevelopment plans are in process that will further transform the city, subsuming existing developments and tying together the various city centre areas, all of which will probably make the seventy-year-old 'Gibson Plan' seem as old-fashioned as the medieval city centre had seemed immediately before the war!

Above: The circular roof of Coventry's indoor market of 1956–57 supports a car park, an innovation at the time. In 2007 IKEA opened its first UK city centre store in Coventry. Unfortunately, in 2020 Ikea announced that the store was to close.

Right: The central 'hub' of the market is here accommodating, appropriately, a roundabout.

This is the view from the 'crossroads' of the Precinct and Market Way towards the Upper Precinct. Despite the original view having been blocked at street level, the old cathedral spire still provides a focal point.

The Cathedral

Perhaps it is the city's new cathedral that is the crowning glory of the post-war era of modernisation. A competition for a building to replace the bombed-out shell of the old cathedral was held in 1950. Architect Basil Spence (best known for his work on exhibition buildings such as 1951's Festival of Britain, and later knighted for his work on the cathedral) was chosen from 200 entries, and his two books about the building – *Out of the Ashes* and *Phoenix at Coventry* – sum up the project. Rather than attempt a rebuilding of the ruins, Spence planned a new building, adjacent and connected to the old by a lofty porch. The foundation stone was laid by the Queen in March 1956, and the cathedral was consecrated in May 1962. A few days later, Benjamin Britten's *War Requiem*, composed for the occasion, was premiered in the building to mark the consecration.

The new cathedral is full of innovative features. Behind the altar is a vast tapestry of Christ designed by Graham Sutherland (at more than 75 feet tall, supposedly the biggest in the world at that time). The lofty outward-curving Baptistery Window, designed by John Piper, comprises 195 panes of coloured glass in rich colours. The 80-foot-high stained-glass windows in the zigzag walls of the nave face away from the congregation, so can only be fully appreciated when one turns and views the interior from the altar end. Also mounted on the smooth sandstone

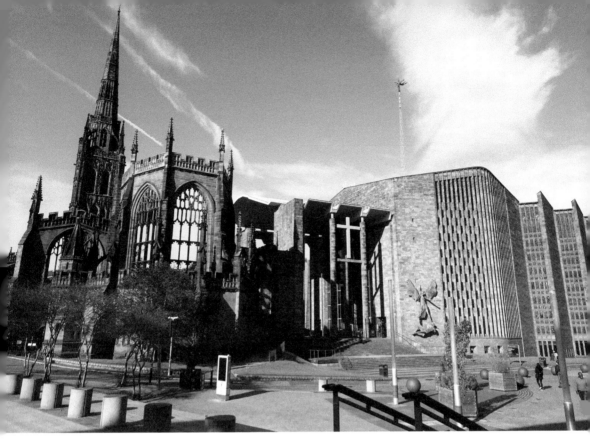

Above: Although perhaps architecturally startling in the early 1960s, the cathedrals old and new now provide a harmonious and iconic picture of the modern city.

Right: An aerial view of the new cathedral from the tower of the old. On the left is the Chapel of Unity, with its slate 'fins'. Note the 'flèche' (a tall slender 'spire' rising from the crossing in the roof at the near end) instead of a conventional tower.

Left: Sir Jacob Epstein's striking sculpture of St Michael and the Devil. Sadly Epstein died in 1959, aged seventy-eight, so did not see his work placed in position in 1960.

Below: The new cathedral's great 'West' window (geographically south) was designed and engraved in situ by John Hutton. His 'Screen of Saints and Angels' is 70 feet high and 45 feet wide. This transparent wall links old and new, each visible from the other – note the reflection.

nave walls are ten stone panels, the 'Tablets of the Word'. These and the baptismal font (made from a boulder from Bethlehem) were designed and carved by the émigré German letter carver Ralph Beyer. The Great West Window, the 'Screen of Saints and Angels', has figures engraved directly onto the glass by John Hutton. On the roof the unconventional spire, or 'flèche' (a spirelet, from the French for 'arrow'), 80 feet (24 metres) tall, was lowered into place by helicopter in April 1962. On the outside east wall adjacent to the Baptistery Window is an enormous bronze statue of 'St Michael's Victory over the Devil' of 1958, by US-born British sculptor Jacob Epstein. ('But he's a Jew,' was an objection to the use of his work. 'So was Jesus,' retorted Spence.)

A recent poll saw the cathedral voted the nation's favourite twentieth-century building. There is obviously far more to see and experience here than can be covered by this book – a visit is strongly recommended.

City of Reconciliation

When Spence first visited Coventry 'I was deeply moved. I saw the old Cathedral as standing clearly for the Sacrifice, one side of the Christian Faith, and I knew my task was to design a new one which should stand for the Triumph of the Resurrection.'

Not surprisingly, there continues to be a strong influence of reconciliation within the theology of the cathedral, represented by the International Centre for Reconciliation, established in 1940 to promote reconciliation in areas of conflict. Its work is continued by the Coventry Cathedral Reconciliation Ministry, 'committed to reconciliation in various situations of violent conflict, some related to religious dispute and others fuelled by different factors'. The ICR also coordinated the Community of the Cross of Nails, an international network of 150 reconciliation organisations in sixty countries.

One moving outcome of this spirit is the twinning of Coventry and Volgograd, the former Stalingrad. In 1942 both Stalingrad and Coventry were being ravaged by war, and a group of city women, including the female mayor, got together to help those similarly suffering in the Soviet Union. Despite the deprivations of wartime, they raised more than £4,000, which was used to buy mobile X-ray units for the Red Army. A tablecloth with the embroidered message 'Little help is better than big sympathy' was sent to Stalingrad – 830 Coventry people paid sixpence each to have their names added.

In return Coventry received an album signed by 36,000 women; tragically, by the time the official 'bond of friendship' was put in place in 1944, only 9,796 Stalingrad citizens had survived the devastation. But Coventry and Volgograd had succeeded in becoming the world's first 'twinned cities'. In 2019 the 75th anniversary of that historic bond of friendship was marked – Coventry now has twenty-six twin towns and cities around the world and is known as a city that welcomes migrants and refugees.

3

Communications

I hope the good people of Coventry will make their streets wider before I come
here again.

Prince of Wales (later George IV), having been stuck in a 'traffic jam' in
Greyfriars Lane in 1807.

Canals and Roads

Coventry's central location made it a crossroads for commerce and communications
from earliest times. The advent of the modern age of transport arrived with
the Coventry Canal, established in 1768 and built primarily to move coal from
collieries in Coventry, Bedworth and Nuneaton to the rest of the Midlands and
beyond. It was engineered by the famous canal builder James Brindley, but within
a year the money ran out, with the canal having only reached Atherstone. It was
finally connected with the Trent & Mersey Canal at Fradley, near Lichfield, in
1789. Although built in sections over a long period of time, today the Canal &
River Trust describes the whole route from Coventry to Fradley as the Coventry
Canal. It is 38 miles long and has thirteen locks.

It connected with the Oxford Canal at Hawkesbury Junction, in the city's
northern outskirts, and with the Ashby Canal north of Bedworth, and thus became
part of an important network of waterways linking Birmingham with London.
From Hawkesbury to Coventry it is known locally as the 'five 'n half', referring to
the mileage from the city centre.

The canal survived serious wartime damage and has always remained navigable.
In 1957 the Coventry Canal Society was established to promote its use and
maintenance. The canal basin at Bishop Street, higher than street level and with
extensive warehouses along adjacent Leicester Row, was restored in 1984 and
features a range of small businesses and some historic canal architecture; there is
also a bronze statue of Brindley.

One of the principal roads through Coventry was the Holyhead Road, which
arose from the development of a new route between London and Holyhead by

Right: The canal grain warehouses above Leicester Row are considerably higher than road level.

Below: James Brindley peruses a plan of the Coventry Canal, with the canal-level warehouses behind.

Thomas Telford in 1815–39. Following the 1800 Act of Union that unified Great Britain and Ireland, it was important that stagecoaches and mail coaches should have speedy access to boats for Ireland from Holyhead. To facilitate this the road was nowhere steeper than 1 in 17 (5.9 per cent), and in Allesley, in Coventry's north-western outskirts, the deep early 1820s cutting that was necessary to keep the road as level as possible is still clear to see. Originally the road had followed the route of the Roman Watling Street (the present-day A5), but Telford's new road was diverted to include the commercial centres of Coventry, Birmingham and Wolverhampton. The first direct Coventry–London coach had begun in 1750, and the city was also linked to Bristol, Leicester and Birmingham. By 1825 a coach leaving Coventry at 11.15 a.m. could reach London that same evening!

What became the A45 was another important road through the city, linking Birmingham with Ipswich and the Suffolk ports. The road originally passed through the city, but was diverted to form part of the city's 6-mile-long southern bypass, a dual carriageway built between 1930 and 1939. In 1959 this was linked to the M45, a spur from the original section of the M1. Effectively the first motorway to serve Coventry, it was followed by the M6 north of the city in 1971, and the M69 to Leicester in 1976. The Coventry Eastern Bypass re-routed the A46 east of the city, linking the M69/M6 and the A45.

Nearer the city, the Ring Road was begun in the late 1950s, and completed between 1962 and 1974. It is a dual carriageway just under 2 miles long tightly

The extent to which Telford lowered the Holyhead Road through Allesley village, north-east of Coventry, to reduce the gradient, is evident here. The view is looking towards the city. The village was bypassed in 1966.

encircling – some might say strangling – the city centre. When first envisaged it was to have parallel cycle paths, broad swathes of parkland on each side and nine roundabout junctions. However, as built it is entirely grade-separated except for one roundabout. By necessity its nine junctions are very close together, 'causing a frenzy of flyovers, underpasses and short sliproads ... frightening but an awful lot of fun!' according to the website Roads.org.

Railways and Trams

Within a decade of Telford's Holyhead Road, in 1838 the railway arrived in Coventry in the shape of the London & Birmingham Railway. (This became part of the London & North Western Railway in 1847, the London Midland & Scottish Railway in 1923 and British Railways upon nationalisation in 1948, these successive companies each enjoying a monopoly of the city's rail services.) The original station was soon rebuilt, with access from Eaton Road. It had two long platforms with 'through roads' in between, and was connected to the city centre by tram. This sufficed until it was completely rebuilt in 1960–62, with the coming of electrification from Euston to Rugby, Birmingham and beyond – and nicely coinciding with the consecration of the new cathedral. The first post-war railway station constructed by British Railways, the listed structure has four platforms and a spacious glazed two-storey-high concourse.

The frontage of Coventry railway station. Pevsner described it as 'One of the best stations of the period in England'.

North from Coventry a branch ran to Nuneaton; opened in 1850, it had to close for three years following the collapse of the lengthy viaduct at Spon End in 1857. The line was a victim of the Beeching era cuts and closed to passengers in 1965; happily, services were reintroduced in 1987, new stations opened and the service much improved, now with through trains from Nuneaton to Leamington Spa. The latter branch, south from Coventry via Kenilworth, was opened in 1851, but also lost it passenger service in 1965; services were reinstated in 1977 following the opening of Birmingham International station, which led to the diversion of some services south from Birmingham via Coventry.

At the time of writing Coventry is well served by CrossCountry, West Midlands Trains and Virgin Trains, with not only local services but through trains on the London–Scotland route.

Coventry's tram system began in 1884 with Coventry & District Tramways, running steam trams from the station to Bedworth. It was electrified in 1895, and further routes opened. In 1912 the trams were taken over by the Corporation, but by the 1930s the system was suffering from bus competition. Ironically, because electricity was easier to source than petrol or diesel, and the deteriorating world situation, the trams soldiered on – only to be abandoned almost overnight following the 1940 Blitz. The track, wires and trams went for scrap.

Coventry Corporation continued to operate buses until 1974, when the operation was taken over by the West Midlands Passenger Transport Executive, then in 1986 by West Midland Travel Ltd. Today bus services are coordinated by Transport for West Midlands, with services operated by a number of companies, notably National Express.

The City at Work

It is to industry that the thriving and prosperous city of Coventry owes its importance.

Coventry Official Guide, 1937

Wool and Weaving

From a small village of perhaps 350 people at the time of the Domesday Book, by the fourteenth century Coventry's population had risen to more than 5,000 adults (ranking with York, Bristol and Plymouth as the four largest cities outside London), and the city's merchants had obtained the privilege of freedom from tolls for all their goods throughout the country, and trade guilds had been established.

The foundation of the city's wealth was wool, together with its central position and tradition of craftsmanship. By the mid-thirteenth century Coventry merchants were selling wool in Leicester; a century later they were converting the wool to cloth, and for 200 years the city was the centre of the cloth industry in the Midlands, involving drapers, weavers, fullers, dyers and tailors; woollen caps were a speciality. By the eighteenth century silk weaving had become the principal activity, supplying a very specialised market for ribbons and the like, which was in great demand for the fashions of the day. Weaving remained essentially a cottage industry, with ribbons produced by outworkers. In 1818 there were more than 3,000 powered looms in the city and some 5,500 handlooms, employing nearly 10,000 people, 4,000 of whom were women and children. By the 1850s the figure was 25,000.

Brothers John and Joseph Cash were responsible for a significant example of this system. Quakers, philanthropists and model employers, they built forty-eight (originally intended to be 100) three-storey weavers' cottages in 1857 in what is now Cash's Lane, beside the Coventry Canal on the northern outskirts of the city. On the top floor of each cottage was a well-lit work area known as a 'top shop', with jacquard looms powered by a central steam engine. The houses still stand, now Grade II listed.

The Quaker Cash brothers' 'cottage factory' in what is now Cash's Lane had accommodation on the lower floors and 'top shops' above, and is now owned by a housing association. The bridge in the foreground spans the Coventry Canal.

The coming of the railway further helped the industry, and until around 1890 five leading London wholesale houses maintained a 'Coventry ribbon department'.

Incidentally, John Cash bought his house, 'Rosehill', from fellow ribbon manufacturer and philanthropist Charles Bray, with whose family novelist George Eliot was staying; her third novel was *Silas Marner: The Weaver of Raveloe* (1861), which, though set earlier in the century, no doubt drew on her knowledge of these weaver outworkers.

Still based in Coventry, Cash's was granted a Royal Warrant in 1964, and, the sole survivor of that industry in the city, has survived thanks to diversifying into a range of quality woven products – including, of course, its famous name labels, which have graced countless thousands of school uniforms.

Another famous name was Coventry-born ribbon-weaver Thomas Stevens (1828–88). In 1860 a free-trade treaty with the Continent increased competition and brought widespread unemployment and hardship, leading to a decline in the domestic industry. However, Stevens experimented with a programmable jacquard loom and began to weave colourful silk pictures, used for bookmarks, greetings cards and the like; business boomed, and his 'Stevengraphs' – eventually numbering 900 different designs – won medals around the world.

Continuing the textile theme, Courtaulds established a factory at Foleshill in 1905, not far from Cash's and again near the Coventry Canal, using largely female labour. Having, like many Coventry weavers, a French Huguenot background, Courtaulds had been established in Essex in the 1790s as a silk, crepe and textile business. By the twentiethth century the company wanted to reduce its dependence on natural silk, and in 1904 acquired the patents to the viscose process for manufacturing artificial silk, or rayon. The firm also claims to have produced the first nylon yarn here in 1941. Courtaulds became the world's leading man-made fibre production company before being broken up in 1990; the imposing landmark of the Foleshill factory, threatened with demolition in the 1990s, has since become an office and technology 'park'.

Clocks and Watches

Meanwhile, in the late seventeenth century the making of clocks and watches began to emerge as an important industry. It was also based on individual makers and assemblers, using, like the weavers, well-lit 'top shops'. Factories were also established, including Rotherham & Sons in Spon Street in 1750, where my maternal great-grandfather worked. Charles Dickens is said to have visited Rotherham's factory in 1857, being presented with a Coventry-made watch. By 1861 more than 2,000 people were engaged in clocks and watches, most around Spon Street, Chapelfields and Earlsdon. It was a very specialised industry – many of the parts hand-made and hand-assembled (by men like my paternal

Rotherham & Sons became known as such in the 1850s, although the firm was much older. This is the firm's premises in Spon Street.

grandfather) – with some 100 processes, including movement-makers, dial-makers, case-makers and engravers. The rough metal parts appear to have come mainly from Lancashire. In 1860 there were ninety watch manufactures in Coventry, with nearly 700 apprentices, but the same free-trade treaty that had decimated the weaving industry had the same effect on watchmaking. Overseas competition from America and Switzerland led to a decline, and although in 1899 Rotherham's was still producing 100 watches a day and employing between 400 and 500 people, with 200 outworkers, the end for most manufacturers was nigh. Happily, the name of Rotherham is still with us; having passed through several owners, Rotherhams 1750 Ltd still manufactures superb timepieces in the city.

In 2002 the Coventry Watch Museum purchased Nos 22, 23 and 24 in Court 7 in medieval Spon Street, an original surviving 'court' built in 1820; the museum houses a huge collection of clockmaking and watchmaking artefacts and information on the industry in Coventry.

Bicycles

With characteristic adaptability, as the weaving and watchmaking industries declined, enterprising individuals saw new ways to occupy the city's skilled craftsmen. One James Starley (1830–81), born in Sussex, came to Coventry in 1861 and set up the Coventry Sewing Machine Co., likely offering employment to out-of-work weavers.

Then in 1868 Starley was asked to undertake the manufacture of a clumsy French 'bone-shaker' bicycle. At once he saw means to improve the machine – with solid rubber tyres and wire-spoked wheels – and the 'penny farthing' bicycle was born. In 1869 Starley set up his own bicycle business and in 1876, to make the new means of transport more accessible, invented the tricycle. This new industry took root in the city, and the 'safety bicycle' – essentially the bicycle we know today – followed in 1884; it used a chain-drive and pneumatic tyres (patented by Dunlop in 1889 and manufactured in Coventry from 1893). By 1890 Coventry-built cycles were being sold around the world. In 1906 Rudge Whitworth, then the world's largest cycle manufacturer, alone produced 75,000 machines, and the city's total output stood at well over 300,000. It also pioneered the 'easy payment' instalment method of paying, and at one time employed around 1,600 workers.

Bicycle entrepreneurs were attracted to the city. The Riley brothers (later of Riley Cars fame) were former ribbon weavers and loom-makers; George Singer (1846–1909) and William Hillman (1848–1921) were both former Starley employees, and subsequently became car manufacturers; and the Sturmey family, of Sturmey-Archer three-speed gears, were also Coventry based. William Iliffe (1843–1917), a Coventry printer, began to produce *The Cyclist* magazine in 1878, in collaboration with Henry Sturmey, and later *The Autocar*. Thomas Humber (1841–1910) arrived from Nottingham, and bicycle-maker Daniel Rudge (1840–80) from Wolverhampton.

Right: The memorial to James Starley, 'Inventor of the Bicycle', on Greyfriars Green.

Below left: 'If you are wise you go to Coventry for cycles and motorcycles', reads the advert for the famous Coventry Eagle cycles. The firm began building bicycles, then tricycles, from the 1890s, assembled from bought-in parts, then motorcycles from 1898.

Below right: Like 'Godiva', 'Three Spires' was an obvious brand name to adopt for Coventry-made products. Walter Greaves was a British cyclist who in 1936 set the world record for distance ridden in a year – 45,383 miles – despite having only one arm and falling off numerous times!

If you are wise you go to Coventry for CYCLES AND MOTORCYCLES —if you are wiser still, you go to COVENTRY — EAGLE *always ahead, always reliable* AND ALWAYS GOOD VALUE

CYCLES from £4-4-0 or 2/- weekly. SILENT SUPERB TWO STROKES from £27-10 or £8-1-3 down. FLYING SERIES (FOUR STROKES) from £47-10 or £13-13-9 down. SILENT PULLMAN TWO-SEATER with Car Sprung Rear Wheel £45-10 or £13-3-9 down. Write for attractive literature to the manufacturers. The Coventry Eagle Cycle & Motor Co., Ltd., Bishopgate Green Works, Foleshill Road, Coventry.

COVENTRY-EAGLE

GREAVES RECORD
£6·2·6
CASH OR 3/- WEEKLY
A Replica of the actual Bicycle which gained for England

The World's Endurance Record
45,383 MILES IN ONE YEAR

Fitted with Tri-Velox Gear & Safety Spokes
ASK YOUR LOCAL DEALER FOR ILLUSTRATED CATALOGUE

PRICES FROM £3·19·9 CASH
OR 2/- WEEKLY

THREE SPIRES
THE WORLD'S BEST BICYCLE REGD.

MANUFACTURED BY
COVENTRY BICYCLES LTD.
OSBORNE ROAD, COVENTRY

'Phone: Coventry 3028   'Grams: Bicycles, Coventry

Unlike the earlier industries, volume production was the key, and factories such as the Rover and Triumph works were established. The Triumph cycle business was sold to Raleigh of Nottingham, which continued to make bikes in Coventry until 1954.

Another important industrial magnate to emerge at this time was Alfred Herbert (1866–1957) from Leicestershire. By the late 1880s he was running a general engineering business in the city; by 1914 he had 2,000 employees, and Alfred Herbert became the largest machine tool firm in England. He was a philanthropic figure and gave land and money to improve his home city, including the endowment of the Herbert Art Gallery & Museum.

Cars

A number of famous names in the automobile world have already been mentioned, so it is no surprise to learn that many bicycle manufacturers evolved into motor car production, via motorcycles. In 1905 there were twenty-two motorcycle manufacturers in Coventry, but following the First World War it was the car that conquered all.

Early on the scene was the Daimler Motor Company Limited, founded in London in 1896, which set up its manufacturing base in Coventry. The first Coventry Daimler-engined car – the first British motor car – emerged the following year, and soon the factory in Sandy Lane, Radford, was producing three of its own craftsman-built cars a week, as well as others under licence; the Daimler was claimed to be the first motor car to go into serial production. Daimler was also the first company to sell a limousine to the royal family. In 1910 the company merged with Birmingham's BSA, then in 1960 it was bought from BSA by Jaguar.

One of Coventry's most famous marques, Jaguar had begun life as the Swallow Sidecar Company in 1922. In 1934 co-founder William Lyons (1901–85) formed S. S. Cars Ltd, and the Jaguar name first appeared as a model name in 1935; ten years later it became the company name. In 1950 Jaguar agreed to lease from the Ministry of Supply the Daimler Shadow 2 factory in Browns Lane, Allesley, and the Daimler name was used for the company's most luxurious saloons.

A chequered history followed. In 1965 Jaguar merged with the British Motor Corporation, which in turn became the unsuccessful holding company British Leyland in 1968. Jaguar's pedigree was being neglected, so in 1984 it was floated off as a separate company, and under Sir John Egan it enjoyed a new prosperity. In 1999 Jaguar became part of Ford, with Land Rover joining in 2000. Under Ford's ownership Jaguar never made a profit, and in 2008 it was announced that India's Tata Group had been a successful bidder for the company, together with the dormant brands Daimler, Lanchester (another Coventry-based manufacturer that had been purchased by BSA in 1930) and Rover. In 2013 the company became Jaguar Land Rover. Happily, while most motor manufacturers have completely disappeared from Coventry, Jaguar still has its international headquarters in the city, at Whitley.

Some famous Coventry marques of bygone years.

By 1931 there were eleven car-producing firms in Coventry, but some forty had opened and closed since 1918. Rudge-Whitworth produced a cycle-car in 1912. Starley's Coventry Machinists produced a cheap car, the Cadet, in the 1920s. Rover produced its first car in 1904, and by 1923 had abandoned bicycles altogether. In 1938 Riley became part of William Morris's Nuffield organisation. Morris (1877–1963), another great philanthropist in the city and elsewhere, had come to Coventry in the 1920s, making engines for cars assembled at Cowley, Oxfordshire.

Meanwhile, brothers William (1894–1964) and Reginald (1896–1977) Rootes were running a successful motor car servicing and distribution business in London, founded in 1913, and in 1928 were keen to produce their own cars. They thus began acquiring some well-known British motor manufacturers, including Coventry's Hillman, Humber (which had once employed W. O. Bentley and Alec Issigonis as engineers) and Singer, as well as Sunbeam-Talbot, Commer (a Humber subsidiary) and Karrier. When the Rootes Group was floated on the Stock Exchange in 1949 it employed 17,000 workers, and had three factories in Coventry.

Problems arose through strikes, undercapitalisation and losses from the Hillman Imp, and from 1964 to 1967 Rootes Motors was progressively taken over by Chrysler; by 1978 what remained of Chrysler UK had been sold to Peugeot and Renault. The principal plant was at Ryton-on-Dunsmore, south-east of the city. The huge site closed in 2006 and the following year was redeveloped for industrial use and completely demolished.

Another name worthy of mention is Armstrong Siddeley. The Siddeley Autocar Company was founded in Coventry by John Davenport Siddeley (1866–1953) in 1902, and was later acquired by Wolseley, and subsequently by Armstrong Whitworth. Armstrong Siddeley built luxury cars in Coventry from 1919 until 1960. (J. D. Siddeley subsequently became the 1st Lord Kenilworth, and purchased Kenilworth Castle for the nation.)

In 1903 the Standard Motor Company was founded in Coventry by Reginald Maudslay (1871–1934). It purchased former bicycle company Triumph in 1945, and in 1959 officially became Standard-Triumph International, with the Triumph name on all its products; the Standard name was last used in Britain in 1963. During the First World War the company built aircraft at its new Canley factory, which opened in 1916 and subsequently became the main centre of operations. This extensive factory is now no more, the site occupied by an industrial estate.

In 1945 Standard announced that it was to manufacture Harry Ferguson's famous tractors, and an Air Ministry shadow factory at Banner Lane, run by Standard during the war, would be used for the project. For many years the 'little grey Fergies' were powered by the Standard Vanguard engine. Standard parted company with Ferguson in 1959, by which time the latter had merged with Canada's Massey Harris and the Ferguson Company to become Massey Ferguson. The company's headquarters have been in Buffalo, New York, since 1997, and it is now part of AGCO.

By 2000 the huge plant was producing more than 70,000 tractors per annum, most for export; however, it was decided that production should be moved to France, and Banner Lane closed in 2002 when the last tractor, number 3,307,996, was completed. The plant has since been demolished and cleared and a housing development called Bannerbrook Park now occupies the site, where there is a memorial to the tractor factory.

Meanwhile the Standard-Triumph company was bought by Leyland Motors in 1960, later British Leyland, and the Triumph or Rover Triumph BL subsidiary used the former Standard factory at Canley in Coventry until it closed in 1980. In 1994 BMW acquired the Standard and Triumph brands following its purchase of BL's successor, the Rover Group, in 1994.

Another company whose products are very familiar, especially to Londoners, was Carbodies, founded in 1919, making bodies for car-makers who lacked the facilities to make their own – including Alvis, located on the opposite side of Holyhead Road.

After the war, Carbodies famously began making the bodies for the Austin FX3 London 'black cab', introduced in 1948, as well as finishing and delivering the complete vehicles; more than 7,000, mostly for London, were produced over ten years. In 1954 the company was acquired by BSA/Daimler, and in 1958 Carbodies began to manufacture the body for and assemble and deliver the Austin FX4 taxi. By the 1980s the FX4 was its only product. In 1992 the company was rebranded London Taxis International, with new and innovative models, making LTI Vehicles a worldwide supplier of London-type taxis. Sadly, in 2012 the company was placed in voluntary administration, but since 2017 has been rebranded as the London EV Company developing electric commercial vehicles, including taxis, at a new plant near Coventry.

In 1921 18,692 people were involved in building cycles and motorcycles; by 1939 the figure for the motor car industry was 38,000, and in 1960 more than 81,000 people were building motor vehicles, tractors and aircraft. Sadly, industrial disputes, quality control issues and increasing foreign competition and recessions meant that the industry declined rapidly and by 1982 unemployment in Coventry was almost 20 per cent.

The glory days of manufacturing may be gone, but the city still produces electronic equipment, machine tools, agricultural machinery, man-made fibres, aerospace components and telecommunications equipment. However, as with most modern cities, its vast, grim factories have given way to bright modern towers accommodating firms engaged in business services, finance, research, design and development, creative industries, logistics and leisure.

Celebrating the city's important association with the motor industry is the Coventry Transport Museum. The first exhibits were acquired in 1937, and the first motor cars in 1952, and the collection has continued to grow ever since. At first housed in the Herbert Art Gallery & Museum, the opening of the present museum in 1980 has allowed this important collection to grow still further.

The Coventry Transport Museum in Millennium Place is acknowledged as one of the finest collections of significant vehicles in the world, and the largest in public ownership.

From 'bone-shaker' bicycles to Richard Noble's record-breaking 'Thrust' vehicles, the fastest on earth, there's lots to see, and plenty of interactive displays.

To demonstrate that the city has not turned its back on the car industry, in 2019 Jaguar Land Rover announced that it would invest millions in the production of electric vehicles in the UK, and £1 billion will be invested in clean-car technology by the Advanced Propulsion Centre … based in Coventry.

The City at Play

At various times some of the great geniuses of the stage have been brought before
Coventry audiences.

Benjamin Poole, *Coventry: Its History and Antiquities*, 1870

Stage and Screen

The city's first permanent theatre was erected in 1819 in the now long-vanished
Smithford Street, featuring a stock company for part of the year. Following a
downturn in popularity, it was modernised in 1857 and became a music hall in
1865. By now known as the Royal Theatre, it changed ownership in 1880, but
was considered too small compared with the same owner's nearby Opera House.
It was renamed the Empire Theatre of Varieties in 1889, but closed in 1895, to be
demolished in 1903.

In 1869, at the city's Britannia music hall, the famous Dan Leno made his first
solo appearance, aged just nine.

The Royal Opera House in Hales Street was built in 1889, with stalls and three
circles to accommodate 2,000 people, and a large stage. Damaged by bombs
during the Second World War, it reopened as a cinema, but did not thrive and
closed in 1961.

Perhaps the city's most famous theatre was the Coventry Hippodrome, which
opened in 1937, the third theatre in Coventry to bear that name and built adjacent
to the second, opened in 1906 in Hales Street. The new theatre was much larger,
with one of the largest stages in the country and almost 2,000 seats in its art deco
interior; for forty years it was the premier pantomime venue in the Midlands.
In 1955 it became simply the Coventry Theatre, dubbed the 'Showplace of the
Midlands', and was occasionally used as an ABC Cinema. In 1979 it was renamed
the Coventry Apollo, but eventually closed in 1985 with a performance by singer
Barbara Dickson, after which it was relegated to becoming a Gala bingo hall.
Sadly this relic of a very different pre-television entertainment age was demolished
in 2002 to make way for the new Millennium Place.

Entertainments. Meetings.

HIPPODROME

HALES STREET, COVENTRY.

WEEK COMMENCING MONDAY, JULY 23rd.

6.45　TWICE NIGHTLY　**8.50**

JOSE BROOKS PRESENTS THE BRILLIANT
UP-TO-DATE REVUE, IN 16 SCENES—

GOING STRONG

ALBERT BRUNO,

THE FAVOURITE REVUE COMEDIAN.

HAROLD MARTYN.　　　　　　EDITH SCOTT.
ARTHUR FILMER.　　　　　EILEEN MOWBRAY.

THE "ROYAL BLUE" QUARTETTE.

RHYS DAVIES.　　　　　　DORIS STONE.
BILLY PHELAN.　　　　　LYDIA WEBBER.

LESTER & TODD.

THE "TREASURE" GIRLS.

GLADYS HAY.

A FEAST OF COMEDY, MUSIC, FUN & BEAUTY.

ALL THE LATEST NEWS ON THE HIPPOSCOPE.

Entertainments. Meetings

EMPIRE THEATRE

COVENTRY.

DURING SUMMER SEASON,
Mondays to Fridays CONTINUOUS PERFORMANCE
from 6.30. Saturdays Twice Nightly at 6.30
and 8.45. Matinees Mon., Thurs. and Sat. at 3.

SUNDAY, JULY 22nd, ONLY,
RENEE ADOREE and CONRAD NAGEL in
HEAVEN ON EARTH.

MONDAY, TUESDAY, AND WEDNESDAY ONLY,
JACK HOLT and DOROTHY REVIER in

THE TIGRESS.

TWO-ACT COMEDY.　　　　PATHE GAZETTE.
ANDY GUMP'S ONIONS. BURNESE OBERLAND.
THURSDAY, FRIDAY, AND SATURDAY ONLY,
ROBERT FRAZER and JOBYNA RALSTON in

THE DESERT PRINCE.

OLD WIVES WHO KNEW, Comedy.
PATHE GAZETTE.　　NEWLYWEDS, Comedy.

Addresses.

RIDGWAYS,

403 & 405, FOLESHILL ROAD,

Programme

COVENTRY THEATRE

Showplace of the Midlands

Week Commencing 15th MARCH, 1965

The
National Theatre

Price One Shilling

Above: The Hippodrome became the Coventry Theatre in 1955. This 1928 newspaper notice advertises a twice-nightly 'brilliant up-to-date revue'. The Empire cinema, in Hertford Street, had been showing films since 1901. *Heaven on Earth* was a silent movie released the previous year. (Author's collection)

Left: In 1965 the Coventry Theatre played host to the National Theatre, with two plays: Noel Coward's *Hay Fever* with Derek Jacobi, and *The Master Builder* with Laurence Olivier and Celia Johnson. (Author's collection)

The Coventry Theatre was demolished in 2002, and the Coventry Transport Museum now occupies the site in Millennium Place, complete with the 'Whittle Arch', a dramatic twin-arch aerofoil-section tubular structure commemorating Coventry-born Sir Frank Whittle and spanning 60 metres.

Coventry's main claim to fame in the theatrical world is the Belgrade Theatre, England's first post-war municipal theatre, built in 1955–58. Its main auditorium is less than half the size of the old Coventry Theatre, but with its new flexible, second space, 'B2', accommodating 250–300, it remains one of the largest regional producing theatres in Britain.

The listed theatre acquired its name in recognition of a gift of Yugoslavian beech from the Serbian capital, which was used in the construction of the auditorium. The Belgrade soon became renowned for staging exciting new drama, and early company members included Ian McKellen, who was given his first professional job here at £8.50 a week, playing as cast with a fortnightly change of play.

The theatre remains the major arts and cultural facility in Coventry and the only building-based professional producing theatre company in the city. It aims to present a broad spectrum of excellent work and produces a wide range of shows. It also started the world's first 'Theatre-in Education' movement in 1965, pioneering new initiatives in community and outreach programmes. In 2007 the theatre was reopened after major refurbishment.

The side of the Belgrade Theatre, England's first post-war municipal theatre, built in 1955–58. The concrete and glass structure accommodates the 'front of house'. Note the city arms. *Inset*: The standard design of Belgrade programme covers in the mid-1960s.

Naturally many famous names have trod the boards in the city's theatres over the years, but it is worth mentioning that one famous double act was formed as a direct consequence of the Coventry Blitz. In 1940 fifteen-year-old Eric Bartholomew and Ernie Wise were touring as solo acts and due to perform in Coventry, but the small digs that Eric's mother Sadie had pre-booked had been damaged in an air raid, so they stayed in Birmingham and commuted to the theatre. After each show they were high on adrenaline, and a desperate Sadie said, 'Why don't you put your brains to some use? Try and do a double act of your own. All you need are a few jokes and a song.' They agreed and decided to split all earnings straight down the middle, settling the momentous deal with just a handshake. Eric later changed his surname to Morecambe, and thus a legendary double act was born somewhere on the railway line between Coventry and Birmingham.

The history of cinemas in Coventry followed a similar course. Moving pictures, shown in theatres and music halls, arrived in the late 1890s, and by 1911 there were five purpose-built cinemas in the city. In the 1930s came the 'super cinemas'; the 2,500-seat Gaumont Palace opened in 1931, the Rex in Corporation Street in 1937 and the Savoy in Radford Road in 1938.

The Rex, which boasted an organ, restaurant and dance floor, was bombed in 1940, the night before *Gone with the Wind* was due to open. Pre-war there were twenty-three cinemas in Coventry, but after the Blitz only seventeen were left.

Then came television, and by the 1980s there were just three; in 1990 only two traditional cinemas were still in operation, before the advent of the 'multiplex' era. Today the Odeon in Croft Road has nine screens, and the Showcase in Walsgrave has fourteen.

Coventry itself has 'starred' in a few notable films. In *The Italian Job* the famous scene of Minis being driven at speed through Turin's sewers was actually filmed in the city in what were then the country's biggest sewer pipes, accessible because they were being installed. The medical TV series *Angels* used the city's Walsgrave Hospital, while the BBC sitcom *Keeping Up Appearances* was shot in the suburbs of Stoke Aldermoor and Binley Woods. Coventry is the setting for the three films in the *Nativity!* series; the first was shot in Coventry during the summer, and local inhabitants decorated the streets to make it look more Christmassy. The films' writer/director Debbie Isitt is a Coventry resident.

An influential musical genre was born in Coventry – 'Two-tone'. Fusing traditional ska with elements of punk and new wave, it took its name from 2 Tone Records, a label founded by Jerry Dammers of Coventry band The Specials (your author played with Jerry Dammers in the King Henry VIII School orchestra in the mid-1960s!). It was Dammers who coined the term, and helped come up with the logo of a man in a black suit, white shirt, black tie, pork-pie hat, white socks and black loafers. Most of the bands considered to be part of the Two-tone genre – including Coventry-formed The Selecter – were signed to 2 Tone Records, which was active between 1979 and 1985. Other long-time Specials members are songwriter and vocalist Terry Hall,

Part of the Specials display in the Coventry Music Museum, packed with fascinating memorabilia. (Courtesy of Coventry Music Museum)

This is the actual organ on which the Specials' *Ghost Town* was written and recorded, on loan from group founder member and keyboard player Jerry Dammers. The song reached No. 1 in the UK charts in 1981. (Courtesy of Coventry Music Museum)

vocalist and rhythm guitar player Lynval Golding, and bass player Horace Panter, and they racked up seven consecutive UK Top 10 singles between 1979 and 1981.

In 2010 the Two-Tone Central museum, café and venue opened in the Coventry University Students' Union building, but in 2011 moved to a hidden gem, the Coventry Music Museum, at Ball Hill, Walsgrave. Packed with Coventry music memorabilia, the 2 Tone/Specials exhibits are particularly fascinating. There is also a gift shop. Well worth a visit!

In 2019 the 40th anniversary of the formation of The Specials was marked by the re-formed band's first new music for thirty-seven years, and a UK tour, including a concert in the Old Cathedral ruins.

Parks and Recreation

Coventry always prided itself on its Parks Department, and today, with increased pedestrianisation of the city centre, there is even more opportunity for trees and flower beds.

COVENTRY WAR MEMORIAL
£5,000 is required
REMEMBER——and GIVE
that their memory may live.

Above left: A postcard inviting subscriptions to support the building of the war memorial. (Author's collection)

Above right: The memorial today. There is, ironically, evidence of bomb damage to the stonework.

The largest and most popular park is the War Memorial Park, known locally as simply the Memorial Park. Conceived in 1919 and opened in 1921, it covers more than 120 acres and is the city's tribute to soldiers who lost their lives during the First World War. Originally Styvechale Common, part farmland and part woodland, it was sold by the Lords of Styvechale Manor as a result of public subscription. Landscaped gardens and sports areas were added, as well as the war memorial itself in 1927.

The memorial stands around 90 feet high, and inside is a room called the Chamber of Silence. Every year on Remembrance Sunday it is open for the public to view the 'Roll of the Fallen', books listing all of the Coventry servicemen who were killed in the two World Wars, as well as more recent conflicts.

The memorial was unveiled by Earl Haig, accompanied by the first Coventry-born winner of the Victoria Cross, Corporal Arthur Hutt, who won the award for his courageous action during the Battle of Passchendaele in 1917. Around the park some 240 memorial trees were planted and dedicated to the fallen, each carrying an identifying plaque; today there are 800.

Another notable city-centre open space that survives today is Greyfriars Green, featured in many old postcards as giving a fine view of the 'three spires',

Above: A plaque from beneath one of the many mature trees commemorating servicemen who lost their lives, in this case Frederick George Smith, a pilot with the Royal Flying Corps.

Left: At the foot of the memorial is a plaque to Private Arthur Hutt VC, the first Coventry-born winner of the Victoria Cross, who was present when the memorial was unveiled.

Above: In the early years of the twentieth century this was the classic view of Coventry and the 'thee spires' from across Greyfriars Green, with Warwick Row on the left and The Quadrant on the right. The cannon in the centre of the Green was a Russian Crimean War example, but was a casualty of the Blitz. (Author's collection)

Below: The similar view today, from the Green, extended towards the ring road, is rather obscured by mature trees, but two of the spires can still be seen.

although today the view is partly obscured by mature trees. The green has an interesting history; 200 years ago it was known as Graffery Muck Hill, comprising a large dunghill of street-sweepings that was auctioned twice a year! Later it was where coachmen washed down their vehicles.

Until 1858 the Coventry Fair was held on Greyfriars Green, then in 1860 the land was sold to the city, provided it maintained and developed it at its own expense, and that there were to be no permanent buildings except statues or monuments, and free access at all times. By 1876 the laying out of the green was complete, boasting a variety of trees, lawns and flower beds. With the construction of the Inner Ring Road, Greyfriars Green was extended to the south over the old line of Warwick Road, and new footpaths now provide a more direct and pleasanter route to the city centre from, in particular, the railway station. The formal reopening of the area took place in 1975.

Another small oasis in the city centre is Lady Herbert's Garden. Industrialist Alfred Herbert has already been mentioned, and he created this beautiful little garden in the 1930s in memory of his second wife, on the site of some of the city's poorest slums. In addition, adjoining the garden he built and endowed two blocks of six almshouses known as Lady Herbert's Homes. The garden incorporates the longest stretch of the old city wall, which he restored.

Another generous gift to the city was £200,000 towards the creation of what became the Herbert Art Gallery & Museum, to be to a design by his cousin, Albert Herbert, begun in 1939. Interrupted by the war, the museum's design was subsequently modified and modernised, and it was built in 1954–60, Alfred Herbert himself laying the foundation stone in 1954 – sadly he died before it was completed. The two large reliefs, 'Man's Struggles', facing Jordan Well, were originally in the Upper Precinct. In 2008 the museum reopened after a £14 million refurbishment, and is now run by Culture Coventry, a registered charity,

These two sculptures by Walter Richie on the side of 'the Herbert' in Jordan Well are entitled *Man's Struggle*. Executed in 1957–59, they were relocated here from the Upper Precinct in 1994.

Above: The modern extension of 'the Herbert' is a glass and laminated timber structure dating from 2006–08.

Below: The 'butterfly-winged' structure of the city's swimming baths dates from 1956, but more modern is the 1970s zinc-clad 'Elephant' leisure centre (left), which spans Cox Street on concrete legs.

which also manages Coventry Transport Museum, the Old Grammar School, and the Lunt Roman Fort outside Coventry at Baginton.

Another legacy of Coventry's rebuilding programme was the new swimming baths, completed in 1965 (four of the city's five baths were destroyed by bombing). It is one of the most spectacular buildings in the city centre, with its birds' wing-style cantilevered roofs. Replacing an original plan for smaller baths around the city, the now Grade II listed three-pool complex was built to contemporary Olympic standards. It is now known as the Coventry Sports & Leisure Centre, under the aegis of the Coventry Sports Trust. The baths are connected to a leisure centre, known locally as 'The Elephant', clad in silver grey zinc sheeting supported on concrete legs over Cox Street.

On the Ball

On the sporting front, Coventry City football club was founded in 1883 by Willie Stanley, who worked for cycle firm Singers; it was consequently known as Singers FC until 1898, when the name was changed to Coventry City. The well-known ground at Highfield Road, in the eastern suburbs, was used from 1899 to 2005. In 1981 it became England's first all-seater stadium.

During that period there were many ups and downs. The team reached Division Two after the First World War, but were relegated in 1925. During the 1930s they enjoyed success, being then nicknamed the 'Bantams'. In 1936 they returned to Division Two, but by 1958 they were down in the newly formed Division Four.

The 1960s was a boom time for the club, under the management of charismatic Jimmy Hill. A new kit brought a new nickname – the 'Sky Blues'. By 1964 they were champions of Division Three, then followed three exciting seasons in Division Two. In 1966–67 the team went twenty-five games unbeaten, leading to Division One.

Hill left to pursue a career in television, and although he returned as Managing Director in 1975, something of the magic had gone. Although in 1987 the Sky Blues battled to win the FA Cup Final, by 1996 another relegation battle loomed, but was avoided. As the club's website says, 'The post Wembley years were dogged by poor signings, sales of their best players, a merry-go-round of managers and empty promises.' Financial problems led to the sale of leading players, but by the end of 2004 the debt still amounted to £23 million, with more cost-cutting required.

In 2003 the City Council approved a new arena project in the north of the city, and the present Ricoh Arena opened in 2005, the UK's first cashless stadium. The 2007/08 season brought the threat of administration, but new investors saved the day. In 2012 the club was relegated to League One, English football's third tier, for the first time in forty-eight years. Financial problems continued, and protracted but unsuccessful talks with the Ricoh Arena meant that the club was forced to look for a temporary home from 2013/14. A deal was announced to share Northampton Town's ground for three years, but in 2014 a deal was agreed and the Sky Blues returned home to the Ricoh. However, sadly, after once more failing to reach an agreement with Ricoh Arena owners Wasps RFC, the club entered a ground-sharing agreement with Birmingham City, so is currently once more homeless.

Some nine years before soccer came to Coventry, in 1874 the first organised game of rugby football was played there, and in the early years the club was very successful, winning the Midland Counties Cup five times. At first playing at the Butts, a temporary home was found on Binley Road before the Coundon Road ground was purchased in 1921, becoming the club's home for more than eighty years. In the 1920s the club produced six England internationals. Wartime brought inevitable disruption, but because so many of the players were engaged in vital engineering work the club survived, and a record seventy-two games were won in succession! In the 1950s Coventry players totally dominated the county side, which saw Warwickshire win the title seven times in eight seasons; in the 1960s 'Cov' was England's premier club, and at one time in the early 1970s thirteen Coventry players were representing England.

Stormy weather: the Ricoh Arena, once home to Coventry City FC, can accommodate 32,000 spectators and is now occupied by Premiership rugby team Wasps. As well as a sporting arena, it also has exhibition and conference facilities.

Above left: Recalling the glory days of the 'Sky Blues' is this statue of Jimmy Hill, who managed the team from 1961 to 1967. Behind him the Wasps celebrate…

Above right: Despite being exiled, the 'Sky Blues' still have a 'Wall of Fame' at the stadium. This is just one of several panels, each featuring bricks that supporters paid for when the club first moved to the stadium in 2005.

The 1980s saw a decline, and in the late 1990s severe financial difficulties hit the club before a rescue package was put together. Sadly, the Coundon Road ground was in need of considerable investment, so the club returned to its origins at the Butts in 2004, yet financial problems persisted. Relegation from the Championship followed, with the club regrouping in National League One for the 2010/11 season, now with part-time players. On the plus side the club has developed a Community Coach programme, in particular among schools and universities, brought about following generous help from sponsors.

Meanwhile Coundon Road was demolished and the site developed as a housing estate with roads named after former prominent players including David Duckham, Bert Godwin and Peter Jackson. (Your author was taught by David Duckham's father at Coundon Junior School in the early 1960s!)

Mention should also be made of 'Coventry Bees', the motorcycle speedway team founded in 1928, with a stadium at Brandon. Sadly, the latter was lost in 2017 when the club had its licence frozen as it was unable to guarantee a full season of league racing. The Bees were reformed to compete in the 2018 National League, with meetings staged at Leicester. Unfortunately they became homeless again in 2019, and Brandon Stadium lies derelict.

Educating Coventry

As a school we were particularly happy. We had no set of rules; Miss Scott insisted only that 'no girl should make a nuisance of herself', which, though seemingly lenient, covers a great deal and is surely the basis of all laws and rules.'
Early recollections from the Stoke Park School magazine
Microcosm, summer 1949

Schooldays

There are more than eighty-five primary schools in Coventry, and more than twenty secondary schools, together with special schools and higher education facilities.

It seems that the monks at Leofric's priory ran a school for poor children, and a grammar school after 1303. A grammar school was also established at Bablake, maintained by the Holy Trinity Guild to teach Latin to the children of guild members. The Charterhouse also seems to have kept a school for poor scholars. After the Reformation two new schools were established – the Free Grammar School (later King Henry VIII) and Bablake School. The former was founded by John Hales, who in return for a somewhat controversial grant of certain former monastic properties around Coventry by the king in 1545, following the Dissolution, was obliged to set up a school. He did so at first in the choir of the church of his Whitefriars Monastery, then from 1557 in the former Hospital of St John, founded in 1155 in what is now known as Hales Street, where the school remained until 1885. In that year it moved to its present location on Warwick Road; built in the popular Victorian Tudor style, its façade survived bomb damage in 1941, but the interior is post-war. The school hall was added in 1951, and in the mid-1990s came a new junior school building and dining hall.

Bablake School as we know it today was founded in 1560, when the old guild buildings in Hill Street (already described) were converted into a hospital and school. It was dependent on charitable gifts until 1563, when Thomas Wheatley, a wealthy former mayor of Coventry, endowed it with much of his estate,

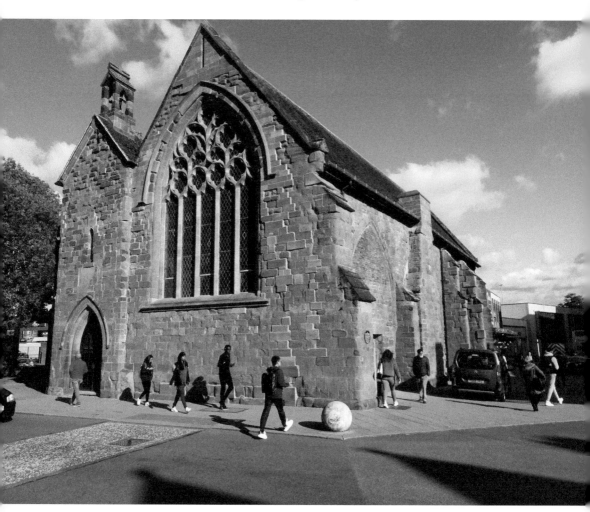

Above: The 'Old Grammar School' in Hales Street. All that remains of the Hospital of St John is this large red-sandstone hall, acquired by John Hales in 1545 and used as a school from 1557 until 1885.

Left: King Henry VIII School moved from Hales Street to these new buildings on Warwick Road in 1885. My father, then a sixth-former, undertook fire-watching duties from the tower during the Blitz.

to accommodate twenty-one boys and a nurse (former pupils are still known as Old Wheatleyans). Very little is known of the school in the seventeenth and eighteenth centuries, and it is said that early in the nineteenth century it had declined to just one boy, but thereafter it began to flourish. In 1855 there were seventy boys, and it was suggested that it might perhaps become a form of 'middle' school between the Coventry Elementary Schools and King Henry VIII, but by 1901 Bablake had amalgamated with three other local charity, or 'gift', boys' schools: Baker, Billing and Crow's School (Black Gift, founded in 1690), Katherine Bayley's Charity School (Blue Gift, 1703) and Fairfax Charity School (Green Gift, 1751). In 1890 the new Victorian school, somewhat similar in appearance to 'Henry's', was opened on its present site in Coundon Road.

Before the war there were around 550 pupils, and Bablake was developing into a grammar school. In 1940 it suffered bomb damage, and was requisitioned as a hostel for building labourers, the school being evacuated to Lincoln, where it stayed until 1943. Bablake became a Direct Grant school in 1957, and in the late 1950s there were further rapid increases in numbers. In 1975 girls were admitted, and around this time it was amalgamated with its former great rival King Henry VIII to form the Coventry School Foundation. Since then the academic results of the combined school have been exceptional.

Bablake School moved from the city out to Coundon Road in 1889. Similar in style to 'Henry's', the buildings are in red brick in late Tudor style.

In order to introduce secondary education for girls, in 1905 it was suggested that King Henry VIII become co-educational, but instead in 1908 the City Council bought Barr's Hill House on Radford Road to become the first general Girls' Secondary School in Coventry. It had been the home of John Kemp Starley, nephew of James Starley, the bicycle pioneer. In 1909 Barr's Hill Guild for former pupils was formed, and still exists with approximately 450 members worldwide.

By 1917 the school had 380 pupils on roll. In 1927 the new wing and covered way from the old house were built, and a new assembly hall in 1936 – this wing is the only building left of the old school today. In September 1939 some girls and staff were evacuated to Leamington and the school cellars prepared as an air-raid shelter. In 1940 the school was bombed and closed for a short while; the new hall was destroyed and seven pupils killed.

By 1945 there were 575 girls on roll, and by 1951 the hall had been repaired. In the 1960s there was much discussion about comprehensive education and the future role of Barr's Hill; the change from grammar school to comprehensive school took place in 1975, when the first boys were accepted. Sadly, extensive rot was found in the old house and, despite many protests, it was demolished in 1981. Today the school is a member of The Futures Trust, a Multi Academy Trust.

Another school with its roots in the cycle industry was nearby Coundon Court. The original house was the home of cycle and car pioneer George Singer, who had the mansion built in 1891. The school opened on the site in 1953 as an all girls' comprehensive school, and became an Academy in April 2012.

Because in 1917 Barr's Hill was very full, Stoke Park school opened to ease the situation (in 1925 it was estimated that the two schools contained 650 girls, instead of 434). It was established in an old house of around 1879 in Bray's Lane known as 'Hope's Harbour'. In 1907 the property was sold and renamed 'Harefield', and twelve years later it became the home of the newly founded Stoke Park Select School for Girls. The school remained there until 1947, when it moved to new purpose-built premises (delayed because of the war) in Dane Road. Stoke Park remained a girls' grammar school until 1975, when boys were admitted to what became a mixed comprehensive school.

The first comprehensives were set up after the Second World War, and Coventry was at the forefront of the movement. The city opened two comprehensives in 1954 by combining grammar schools and secondary modern schools; these were Caludon Castle and Woodlands. Caludon Castle itself is a thirteenth-century Grade I listed ruin, all that remains being a large fragment of sandstone wall, most of the building having been demolished in the eighteenth century. Much of the associated park has been given over to housing. Built as a boys' comprehensive, in 1985 it became co-educational, and in 2004 was designated a Business and Enterprise College. The 1950s buildings were demolished and the school totally rebuilt. It is the lead school in the Castle Phoenix Teaching School Alliance.

Woodlands School was also a boys' comprehensive, and unlike other schools in the city was built around the 'house' principle, which helped with the pastoral care

All that remains of Caludon Castle is this early fourteenth-century fragment and portions of moat.

and teaching of the more than 1,000 pupils. In the 1960s the school's emphasis on 'mixed ability' teaching kept it in the headlines, and it was regularly visited by interested politicians and educationalists. In 2016 the Woodlands Academy (so designated in 2011) was amalgamated with Tile Hill Wood School and Language College to become the West Coventry Academy.

A school with a history stretching far back before the academy era is the Blue Coat Church of England School, now a specialist Music, Maths and Science college. It was founded in 1714 as a school for girls and was located close to Holy Trinity church in the city centre. It was rebuilt in the Gothic style in 1856–57 upon the remains of the north-west tower of Coventry's original cathedral, St Mary's – the tower had survived into the seventeenth century and had then been rebuilt as a house. The buildings were refurbished in 2000 as part of the city's Phoenix initiative and are now the Holy Trinity Church Centre, Blue Coat having moved to its present site in Terry Road in 1964. With a roll of around 1,460 pupils, it is one of very few specialist music colleges in the country, and has close ties with the cathedral, holding several services there every year.

Further Education

The early years of the twentieth century saw important developments in what we would now call further education. A School of Design had opened in 1843, focussing on the ribbon industry. The Mechanics' Institution was formed in 1829 to educate young weavers, and in 1855 it united with the Religious & Useful Knowledge Society to form the Coventry Institute. In 1863 a School of Art was opened in Ford Street. In 1888 the Coventry Institute merged with the Technical Institute to become the Technical College in The Butts. A new building was opened there in 1935 by the future King George VI. The 'Tech' merged with Tile Hill College in 2002 to create City College Coventry.

A need for higher technical training resulted in the Lanchester College of Technology of 1961, which would ultimately become Coventry University. In 2007, the college began the move to a new purpose-built complex in the Swanswell area. In 1970 the Coventry College of Art amalgamated with the Lanchester (and the Rugby College of Engineering Technology) to form the Lanchester Polytechnic (named after automobile pioneer Dr Frederick Lanchester, whose cars were built at the Daimler factory). In 1987 the name changed to Coventry Polytechnic and in 1992 the university was set up under UK government legislation. The Lanchester name has been preserved in the title of the university's art gallery, as well as in the Lanchester Library. The university's logo is the phoenix, representing the rebuilding of the city following the devastation of the Blitz.

The much-admired Coventry Technical College – 'the Tech' – in The Butts was opened by the future King George VI in 1935. Part is now a Premier Inn, but the Tech's art deco Great Hall has been saved as The Albany Theatre, which reopened in 2013, run by a charitable trust.

This evocative statue by Philip Bentham stands in Priory Street near the main entrance to Coventry University. Called *Coventry Boy*, the plaque reads 'This boy has no name but represents all boys of all time who are proud to belong here reaching out as always from rough spun to close weave for family and for city' – a fine sentiment for any further education. It was unveiled in 1966.

This very modern university has opened several new campuses since 2010, including Coventry University London, CU Coventry and CU Scarborough. In 2018 the university marked the 175th anniversary since the founding of the School of Design back in 1843, and the university was a principal partner in Coventry's successful bid to become UK City of Culture in 2021, heralding a programme of exciting events and projects.

In 2019 Coventry University ranked thirteenth, and the country's top modern university, in the Guardian University Guide. In that year the Times and Sunday Times Good University Guide described it as 'one of the most innovative modern universities, bold with its vision of what the 21st century student experience should be'.

The nearby University of Warwick is, despite its name, actually on the outskirts of Coventry. A concept design was produced in 1958, but only in 1961 did planning begin in earnest. It gained its charter in 1965, one of six new universities to be authorised by the Macmillan government. Lord Rootes was to have been the first chancellor (he died before the university was competed) – yet another link between manufacturing and education in the city.

In 2019 the university had more than 26,500 full-time students and almost 2,500 academic and research staff. It includes the Warwick Arts Centre, a multi-venue arts complex in the university's main campus, the largest venue of its kind in the UK outside London. The university consistently ranks in the top ten of all major British universities, and in 2017 was named as the university with the joint second highest graduate employment rate of any UK university (together with St Andrews).

Libraries

Coventry's first public library was the result of the generosity of one of the great city benefactors, John Gulson, mayor in 1867–68. He gave both the site (formerly the old city gaol) and most of the money to establish a library nearly Holy Trinity church in 1873; he added a reference library in 1890. In 1917 the Central Library was renamed the Gulson Library in his honour. It was badly damaged in the Blitz, and partially restored. A new modern library was opened in 1967, and the Victorian building was demolished to make way for the Cathedral Lanes shopping centre. Twenty years later the library moved again to a new and somewhat unlikely city centre location – the former Locarno Ballroom of 1958–60 in Smithford Way. When the dance hall was sold by Mecca, its original owners, it became Tiffany's nightclub and concert venue and hosted some of the best-known bands of the late 1970s – the then little-known Pete Waterman was a DJ there. It closed in 1981 and lay empty until converted for library use. The revolving stage and sprung dance floor were removed, and the original external glass stair tower and bridge entrance were demolished. Reflecting Coventry's multi-cultural status, the library contains books in Bengali, Chinese, French, German, Gujarati, Hindi, Italian, Polish, Punjabi, Spanish, Urdu and Vietnamese; there are also fifty computers with internet access.

Another great benefactor, though not a citizen of the city, was philanthropist Andrew Carnegie (1835–1919), who had left his native Scotland for the USA at the age of twelve and made his fortune in steel. During the last eighteen years of his life he gave away $350 million, much of it to build libraries. In 1910 he offered Coventry £10,000 to establish libraries in Stoke, Earlsdon and Foleshill, which opened in 1913. In recognition of his generosity he was made a Freeman of the city in 1914.

Earlsdon Library, one of three in the city established in 1910 thanks to the generosity of philanthropist Andrew Carnegie.

Celebrated Coventrians

'Why, Coventry!' I exclaimed. 'I was born here.'
Philip Larkin, *'I remember, I remember'*

Benefactors and Martyrs

Perhaps the earliest and most celebrated Coventrian, whose name is still widely used as a symbol of Coventry as much as the celebrated 'three spires', is Lady Godiva (in Old English Godgifu or Godgyfu). She was the wife of Leofric, Earl of Mercia, and they were both generous benefactors to religious houses. In 1043 they founded and endowed a Benedictine monastery in Coventry, as well as endowing and granting land to religious houses elsewhere in the country, making them among the most generous of Anglo-Saxon donors prior to the Norman Conquest.

Today she is best remembered for the legend of her ride, naked and covered only by her long hair, through the streets of Coventry, possibly accompanied by two knights – although the story was first recorded in the thirteenth century, some two centuries after her death. In the traditional version of the story, Lady Godiva takes pity on the city's people, who are suffering from her husband's harsh taxes. She pleads over and over again for Leofric to relax this burden, but he refuses – until at last he will grant her request if she will strip naked and ride on horseback through the city's streets. This she agrees to do, as long as the citizens stay indoors and close all doors and windows – in a seventeenth-century version to 'shutt their dore, & clap their windowes downe'. One theory is that she rode wearing just a shift, an item of underwear, in the mode of a penitent, or she rode stripped of her finery and jewellery, the trademarks of her class. The event is not supported by historical records, and does not fit with what is known of Leofric's character, but perhaps stands as an allegory for the need to help those in need, whatever the cost.

All but one of the citizens complied – the now infamous 'Peeping Tom', a Coventry tailor, although he entered the story much later. As a result of his transgression, so the story goes, he was struck blind – or the townspeople took the matter into their own hands and blinded him.

Above left: The 1949 statue of Lady Godiva in Broadgate by Sir William Reid Dick, bearing a quotation from Tennyson's poem *Godiva*.

Above right: This effigy of Peeping Tom looked down from the top storey of the King's Head Hotel on the corner of Smithford Street and Hertford Street in Broadgate from 1813. The building was destroyed in the Blitz. (Author's collection)

Whatever the truth or otherwise of the legend, a Godiva procession is said to have taken place since at least 1678, in which year a boy enacted the role. Although it raised money for charity, in the early twentieth century it was condemned as 'vulgar', 'sensual and devilish'. It was subsequently superseded by the Coventry Carnival, but in 1997 was revived. In 2003 the carnival and procession were combined to become the Godiva Carnival Procession, associated with the three-day Godiva Festival held in the Memorial Park.

Leofric died in 1057 and was buried in St Mary's Priory and Cathedral. Godiva lived on until, according to one source, 1067, just after the Conquest. She is named in the Domesday Book as one of the few, and the only female, Anglo-Saxon landholders.

Interesting examples of how her name still resonates is the Godiva Chocolatier brand of Belgian confectionary since 1926, and that since 1903 four railway locomotives have been named after her, the most recent being the naming of a Virgin Trains Class 390 'Pendolino' electric multiple unit set *Lady Godiva* in early 2019. The name was chosen following a competition on BBC Radio Coventry & Warwickshire.

Another important Coventry benefactor was successful London cloth merchant Sir Thomas White. Although not a Coventrian (he was born in Reading in 1492), for almost 500 years his wealth has benefitted the city. His wealth led to

Miss Muriel Mellerup of Gloucestershire rides as Lady Godiva in the procession of June 1929, the first non-actress to play the part. Many extra trains and buses were put on for the event, which ended with a pageant in the recently opened War Memorial Park. (Author's collection)

his founding of St John's College, Oxford, endowing it with fifty scholarships, including two for Coventry, where he had presumably done successful trading. In 1542 he purchased land and property in the city for £1,400, including St Mary's Hall, the interest from which was to be distributed among twelve poor men, and to four city freemen and apprentices. In the ensuing years the value of this interest grew, as did the gifts, and it became Coventry's most important charity; by 1851 the charity estate had a surplus of £18,000. Today his benefaction survives in the form of the Sir Thomas White Loan Charity, which provides interest-free loans of up to £20,000 for young businesses in need of investment and up to £10,000 for education, to help young people establish themselves in their chosen career.

Another Coventry luminary from this period is John Thornton, a master glazier and stained-glass artist who produced some of the finest English medieval glass of the early fifteenth century. It has been said that he was the son of a glazier in the royal glass-painting workshops at Westminster in the mid-fourteenth century, and may have assisted his father with windows at Windsor Castle for King Edward III. In 1405 he was contracted by the Dean of York Minster to glaze the minster's famous Great East Window; York's Archbishop at the time was a former Bishop of Lichfield and Coventry, and the window was funded by a former Bishop of Coventry. The east window is the largest in the minster and contains around 1,680 square feet (156 square metres) of glass; it was stipulated that the work should be done by his own hand, but he probably recruited local glaziers, and his style quickly became dominant in the north of England. Other examples of his work are to be found in St Mary's Hall in Coventry, and the old cathedral; the latter pieces were removed before the Blitz and have been preserved.

The statue of Sir Thomas White on Greyfriars Green.

Less happily, we should remember the Coventry Martyrs, who were a disparate group of Lollards, originally followers of John Wyclif, a fourteenth-century religious reformer who criticised the wealth and power of the Church and instituted the first English translation of the Bible. A dozen Coventry people – men and women, humble shoemakers, glovers and hosiers – were burned for 'heresy' in the city between 1512 and 1522, and others in 1555, when the well-known Laurence Saunders met his death 'being fastened to the stake, and fire being put to him, full sweetly he slept in the Lord' (Fox's *Book of Martyrs*). Eleven of them are commemorated by a monument in a public garden in the city between Little Park Street and Mile Lane, while some Cheylesmore streets are named after them.

Arts, Sciences and Statesmanship

Jumping ahead to the nineteenth century, industrial pioneers such as James Starley, the sewing machine and 'safety bicycle' pioneer whose nephew started the Rover car company, have already been mentioned, as have other significant figures in the burgeoning motor car industry.

A man not so far mentioned is Francis Skidmore (1817–96), a prominent metalworker who was born in Birmingham and moved to Coventry in around 1822, possibly because it was an important watchmaking centre. He learned metalworking from his father, undertaking a seven-year apprenticeship with him.

In 1845 they registered as silversmiths, their output consisted primarily of church plate, including chalices, some for the city's St John the Baptist Church. Other high-profile commissions included the glass and metal roof of Oxford's Natural History Museum, and London's Albert Memorial. In Holy Trinity church, Coventry, some of his ironwork, wooden pews and gas lamp standards are still in place. He exhibited at the Great Exhibition of 1851, which helped to stimulate and expand his business.

Skidmore was very much influenced by the Gothic Revival, incorporating medieval designs and styles; he became associated with the famous Gothic Revival architect Sir George Gilbert Scott, and together they worked on screens in Lichfield, Salisbury and Hereford cathedrals. In 1967 Coventry's Herbert Art Gallery bought the latter screen and it was dismantled and removed from the cathedral. However, it was too big to be displayed in Coventry, so in 1983 it was transferred to the Victoria & Albert Museum, where the restoration of its almost 14,000 pieces was at the time the largest conservation project undertaken by the museum.

Sadly, later in life Skidmore's eyesight began to deteriorate, and he spent his last years in poverty in Eagle Street, Coventry.

The Great Exhibition of 1851 was, of course, held in what became dubbed the 'Crystal Palace', the brainchild of another celebrated Coventry citizen, Joseph Paxton (1803–65). Born in Bedfordshire, he began life as a gardener, and by 1823 was working at the Horticultural Society's Chiswick Gardens, close to Chiswick House, home of the 6th Duke of Devonshire. The duke had soon offered the twenty-year-old Paxton the position of head gardener at his famed Derbyshire house at Chatsworth, which featured one of the finest landscaped gardens of the time. Paxton enjoyed a friendly relationship with the duke, who recognised his talents and aided his rise to prominence.

In 1832 Paxton developed an interest in the Chatsworth greenhouses, and designed one with a roof that would be at right angles to the morning and evening sun, and an ingenious frame that admitted maximum light – the predecessor of the modern greenhouse. He also designed a building to accommodate a huge water lily, and was inspired by the structure of the plant's huge leaves – a rigidity provided by radiating ribs connected to flexible cross-ribs – to develop a building structure that he tested by floating his daughter Annie on a leaf. Following further experimentation, he incorporated the idea into his design for the Crystal Palace. It was a revolutionary design in its modular, prefabricated structure and its use of glass.

He remained the head gardener at Chatsworth until 1858, but his connection with Coventry is that in 1845 he was invited to lay out one of the country's first municipal burial grounds. This became the city's London Road Cemetery, and it contains a memorial to him. He was also the city's Liberal MP from 1854 until his death in 1865, among many other public positions and architectural commissions around the country.

The Italianate Lodge and Prospect Tower at the gates of London Road Cemetery. The monument to Joseph Paxton can be seen beyond the entrance.

Coventry was the birthplace of the father of the jet engine, Frank Whittle. He was born on Newcombe Road, Earlsdon, in June 1907. When he was nine the Whittles moved to Leamington Spa, when his father, an accomplished engineer and mechanic, bought an engineering company, which comprised a few lathes and a single-cylinder gas engine, on which young Frank became an expert, alongside an early interest in aviation.

At first he was considered not tall enough to join the RAF, but in 1923, at his third attempt, he was accepted as an apprentice, eventually qualifying as a pilot officer in 1928. He could see that in the future aircraft would have to fly faster, and therefore at higher altitudes, where air resistance was lower. His first thoughts centred on rocket propulsion or gas turbines driving propellers. He then considered using a gas turbine-driven fan enclosed in the fuselage to generate a fast flow of air to propel the aircraft at high altitude. The Air Ministry turned down the idea, so he patented it himself.

In 1935, with RAF approval, he obtained financial backing and formed Power Jets Ltd. Eventually Air Ministry backing allowed further development and an aircraft made a test flight in May 1941; in time this became the Meteor, operational from 1944.

The jet engine was a huge success, especially in the USA. Whittle retired from the RAF in 1948 as an Air Commodore, and was knighted the same year. He then went to work in America, becoming a research professor at the US Naval Academy at Annapolis, and died there in 1996, aged eighty-nine. A statue to him can be found in Millennium Place, outside Coventry's Transport Museum; it was unveiled in 2007 on the centenary of his birth.

Architect Frederick Gibberd was born in Coventry just a year after Whittle, in 1908, and just a stone's throw away in Spencer Avenue, although the family later moved to No. 15 Clarendon Street, where Frederick grew up. His father ran a gentlemen's outfitters business, and Frederick was educated at King Henry VIII School. In 1925 he was articled to a firm of Birmingham architects. He then moved to London working for an architects' practice designing municipal buildings in a modernist/neoclassical or art deco style.

He set up his own practice in 1930, and became involved in the Modern Architectural Research Group, which hoped to promote modernism in Britain. As an enthusiastic modernist, the principles adopted by MARS would have a profound effect on Gibberd's early career. He became established as an influential architect of flats, being co-author of the 1937 book *The Modern Flat*. He was also influential in the design of prefabricated houses, which were used extensively in the rebuilding of Coventry after the war.

He was consultant architect planner for the Harlow New Town development, and spent the rest of his life living in the town he had designed; Harlow is regarded as the most successful of the post-war new towns, and is an object lesson in modern architecture and town planning.

Looking skyward – Faith Winter's 2007 statue of Sir Frank Whittle in Millennium Place.

Gibberd's other major achievements include the Roman Catholic cathedral in Liverpool, the Metropolitan Cathedral of Christ the King, nicknamed 'the Mersey Funnel' from its futuristic conical shape; it is the largest Catholic cathedral in England. Gibberd died in January 1984 at the age of seventy-six, but the Frederick Gibberd Partnership is still active in London.

Coincidentally, another architect who had a more profound effect on Coventry itself was also born in 1908, but this time educated in Manchester. This was Donald Gibson, the city's first City Architect and Planning Officer, who was instrumental in the post-war redevelopment of the city centre following the Blitz. But it was some years before 1940 that Gibson was already planning the new city centre. He was appointed at just twenty-nine, and by the end of the 1930s was developing his radical plan to separate motor traffic and pedestrians, sweeping away the old, cramped medieval streets.

As it happened, the Blitz did the clearance work for him, and in 1946 a levelling stone was placed at the head of what would be the new Precinct. The City Council presented the 'Gibson Plan' – a template for city planning of the future – to the government in 1951. It was said of him, 'He was ahead of his time. What he did astonished the world. Coventry desperately needed his inspiration.'

Gibson left Coventry in 1955 to become County Architect in Nottinghamshire. He was subsequently knighted and became the government's senior architect, responsible for raising architectural standards. He was president of the Royal Institute of British Architects in 1964–65.

At this point it might be worth celebrating another 'architect', but this time of nations rather than buildings. Henry Parkes was born in Moat House Cottage, Canley, in 1815, his father a tenant farmer on the Stoneleigh Abbey Estate. Forced off their farm in 1823 by debt, the family moved to South Wales, then Birmingham, where Thomas did a succession of menial jobs. He married in 1836 and, unable to prosper in England, they decided in 1839 to leave for New South Wales, Australia, as bounty migrants, condemning a society through whose injustices people like him 'are compelled to seek the means of existence in a foreign wilderness'. He told his family of his certainty of 'making my fortune and coming back to fetch all of you'.

In this new world he tried various enterprises, but they failed. However, despite his lack of formal education, he developed talents as a writer, and took an interest in political issues, particularly the growing movement in the colony for self-governance, and universal suffrage. By 1850 he was running a newspaper that supported more rights for the people, and was soon elected to parliament because of his support for democracy. He was premier of New South Wales five times, then in 1889 he declared that the colonies should not just cooperate, but should form a strong new nation; the convention that he organised met in 1891, and gave birth to the Commonwealth of Australia. In 1901, five years after Parkes's death in 1896, Australia at last became a federation, so it is not surprising that he was dubbed 'the Father of the Federation', and *The Times* described him as 'the most commanding figure in Australian politics'.

This great statesman is marked in his native city by Sir Henry Parkes Road in Canley and the former Sir Henry Parkes School. In 2015, to mark Parkes's bicentenary, the Australian High Commissioner visited both Stoneleigh and Coventry to unveil a commemorative plaque at Moat House Cottage.

While on the subject of politics, it is worth mentioning that the well-loved Labour politician Mo Mowlam had strong Coventry connections. Marjorie Mowlam was born in Watford in 1949 but grew up in Coventry, where her father rose to become the city's assistant postmaster. She would later be awarded the Freedom of the City in 1999. Initially educated at Chiswick Girls' grammar school in West London, she later moved to Coundon Court school. One of the most popular of the 'New Labour' politicians, and instrumental in the negotiations for the 1998 'Good Friday Agreement', she very sadly died of a brain tumour in 2005, aged only fifty-five.

Page, Stage and Screen

Probably the most famous novelist to have been associated with Coventry is George Eliot, who was educated in the city and met people there who would be most influential in her future career as a writer. She was born Mary Ann Evans in 1819 on the Arbury Hall estate in Nuneaton, where her father was estate manager. After some basic education, encouraged by her father and unusual for girls at that time, in 1832 she moved to a boarding school in Coventry, in the house 'Nant Glyn' at No. 29 Warwick Row, overlooking Greyfriars Green. Here she did well, but had to leave in 1835 to return to Griff House, the family home near Nuneaton, to help nurse her ailing mother.

Mary Ann's father retired in 1841 and the two of them moved to Coventry, to a fine semi-detached house in Foleshill Road, named 'Bird Grove'. The house is now in George Eliot Road, and at the time of writing lies empty, although it is hoped that it can be rescued and its association with the famous novelist celebrated. She became friendly with Charles and Cara Bray, who lived at Radford, and it was they who opened her mind to fresh and exciting ideas and intellectual pursuits.

In 1849 her father died, leaving her still single but with an income of £90 a year. This needed to be supplemented; she had written articles for the *Coventry Herald* newspaper owned by Charles Bray, but decided that she must move to literary London to make a new life for herself. There Marian Evans, as she now styled herself, emerged as George Eliot, encouraged by her new partner in life, George Henry Lewes. Her rise to become one of the most celebrated novelists of the nineteenth century is beyond the scope of this book, but in 1871/72 her novel *Middlemarch* was published. Considered by many as the finest novel in the English language, in this 'Study of Provincial Life' the town of Middlemarch is supposedly based on Coventry, and her experiences there. Also, Coventry's St Mary's Hall features in one of her other great novels, *Adam Bede*, and was the venue for the

Above: 'Nant Glyn', No. 29 Warwick Row, was the school that Mary Ann Evans (later to become George Eliot) attended from 1832 to 1835.

Below: 'Bird Grove', now surrounded by Victorian terraced houses in George Eliot Road, Foleshill, was the future novelist's home with her father from 1841 to 1849. It currently (2020) stands empty and forlorn, but there are hopes that it can be revived.

George Eliot Fellowship's annual luncheon in 2019 to celebrate the bicentenary of the novelist's birth. George Eliot died in London in 1880. In Nuneaton a hospital, hospice and school are named after her.

A more recent literary Coventrian in the poet Philip Larkin (1922–85). He was born in Poultney Road, Radford, but when he was five years old he moved to a large three-storey house, complete with servants' quarters, in Manor Road; unfortunately this house was demolished in the 1960s to make way for the new ring road. Larkin's father had risen to be the City Treasurer. An unusual figure, he combined a love of literature with an enthusiasm for Nazism.

At first Larkin was an isolated individual, educated at home by his mother and sister, but when he joined the King Henry VIII Junior School he blossomed and made many close friendships. He also developed a passion for jazz. In 1940 he went to St John's College, Oxford, to read English.

After an eminent career as author, poet and librarian, notably at Hull University, and having developed his famously curmudgeonly persona (he turned down an OBE in 1968 and the chance to become Poet Laureate in 1984), he died from cancer in 1985, at the age of sixty-three, and was buried at Cottingham municipal cemetery near Hull. It is interesting that the two places with which Larkin is most associated have been given 'City of Culture' status.

Fond of a drink himself, it is perhaps appropriate that a Coventry city centre pub, the former Tally Ho, Wine Lodge, Eagle Vaults and Tudor Rose, was renamed The Philip Larkin in the poet's honour in 2017.

It is perhaps a lesser-known fact that the great novelist E. M. Forster (1879–1970) ended his days in Coventry. He wrote to great acclaim the novels *A Room with a View*, *Howards End* and *A Passage to India* in his twenties, but wrote no other novel in the second half of his life. During his youth he had been suppressing his homosexuality, but his sexual awakening in his late thirties led to a series of romances with working-class men, which seemed to sap his literary creativity. His only novel about homosexual relationships, *Maurice*, was written in 1914 but not published until after his death.

Following the death of his mother in 1945 Forster lived alone in London and Cambridge but maintained close friendships with a number of men, including a married London policeman called Robert Buckingham. Buckingham later joined the Coventry force, and his wife May came to understand and accept her husband's relationship with Forster. When Forster suffered his final stroke in Cambridge in 1970, May and Bob brought him to their home in Salisbury Avenue, Coventry, and nursed him till the end. A sign affixed to the wall above the garage door marks the centenary of his birth, and his ashes are scattered in the garden.

An author who will be familiar to older readers is Angela Brazil (1868–1947) (pronounced 'Brazzle'), who was one of the first writers of 'modern' schoolgirl stories, intended primarily as entertainment rather than moral instruction. In the first half of the twentieth century she published nearly fifty books of girls' fiction. Her first was *A Terrible Tomboy* (1905), and the most popular *The Nicest Girl in The School* (1909), which sold more than 153,000 copies. Born in Preston, she moved with her brother to Coventry, to No. 1 The Quadrant, in 1911, where they were joined by her sister Amy upon their mother's death in 1915. She became a well-known hostess in Coventry high society and was very interested in local history; although she never married and had no children of her own, she also hosted many children's parties. She was a collector of early children's fiction, and her collection is now in the city's library.

A more recent Coventry author is Susan Hill. She was born in 1942 in Scarborough, but in 1958 her family moved to Coventry, where her father worked in car and aircraft factories; she was a pupil at Barr's Hill School before taking an English degree at King's College, London. Her first novel was published during her first year at university, and was criticised by the *Daily Mail* for its sexual content, having been written by 'a schoolgirl'. Having enjoyed a long and distinguished literary career, she is perhaps best known for her novel *The Woman in Black* (1983), which has been turned into a long-running stage play as well as a TV film.

Writer James Dover Grant was born in Coventry in 1954. Don't recognise the name? He is better known as thriller novelist Lee Child, author of the 'Jack Reacher' books. He wrote his first novel, *Killing Floor*, in 1997. His family relocated to Handsworth Wood, Birmingham, when he was four; there he attended primary school, and eventually King Edward's School. He now lives in New York.

Another writer less well known these days is Paul Jennings, grandson of a Coventry watchmaker, born in Leamington Spa in 1918 and educated at

THE QUADRANT

BUILT CIRCA 1860. COVENTRYS FINEST
EXAMPLE OF TERRACED HOUSING FOR
THE PROSPEROUS MIDDLE- CLASSES OF
THAT ERA. THE NEO-CLASSIC TERRACE
IS BUILT IN SIX INDIVIDUAL SECTIONS
EACH WITH ITS OWN VARIATION
IN DESIGN.

ANGELA BRAZIL

CHILDREN'S WRITER
.
LIVED AND WORKED HERE
1911 - 1947

A plaque recording Angela Brazil's
occupancy of No. 1 The Quadrant.

King Henry VIII School. He went on to write witty essays for many publications, including *Punch*, and became the *Observer*'s first humour columnist, with his 'Oddly Enough' feature. His obituary in 1989 described him as a 'humorist in the best English tradition'. A favourite of your author, his many volumes of published humorous essays are sometimes to be found in second-hand bookshops – seek them out!

Charles Bray's *Coventry Herald* newspaper has already been mentioned, and there was also the *Coventry Standard*, both long-established. A printer's son called William Iliffe decided that the town needed something more up to date, so purchased the *Coventry Times* in 1879, then in 1891 brought out an evening paper, *The Midland Daily Telegraph*, the city's first daily paper. In need of an assistant editor, he appointed Alfred Harmsworth, later Lord Northcliffe and the founder of the *Daily Mail* and *Daily Mirror*.

Today's direct successor to the *Midland Daily Telegraph* is the *Coventry Telegraph*. It became the *Coventry Evening Telegraph* in 1941, then the *Coventry Telegraph*, a morning paper, in 2006. It is now part of the Trinity Mirror Group.

Twentieth-century Coventry produced a good number of celebrities from the world of pop and television. Well-loved radio presenter Brian Matthew was born in the city in 1928. He had musical parents; his father was a conductor of the Coventry Silver Band and his mother a professional singer. He was educated at Bablake School.

In 1934 singer Vincent 'Vince' Hill was born in Holbrooks. He first sang professionally in a pub in Margate when he was just fifteen. He went on to have a string of hits in the 1960s, the biggest being *Edelweiss* (No. 2 in the charts) and *Roses of Picardy* (No. 13), both in 1967. He also released twenty-five studio albums, and at eighty-five was still going strong in 2019!

In 1937 Frank Ifield was born in Coundon to Australian parents. They had travelled to England in 1936, where his father was an inventor and engineer, and creator of the Ifield fuel pump for Lucas Industries, which was used in jet aircraft. The family returned to Australia in 1948 but, already an established musician, Frank returned to the UK in 1959. In 1962–63 he had four UK chart-toppers, including the famous yodelling *I Remember You*. In later years, in 1986, he contracted pneumonia, which led to the loss of part of a lung; as a result he was unable to sing – or yodel – for some years. In 1988 he returned to Australia, where he lives with his second wife.

Record producer Tony Clarke is a Coventrian, born in the city in the midst of the war in 1941. He is best remembered as one of the architects of symphonic 'Prog Rock' through his work with the Moody Blues. He worked with them from 1966, when their fortunes were fading after their first major hit, *Go Now*. He produced their 1967 'symphonic rock' album, *Days of Future Passed*, and their next six albums, helping them develop a complex sound, using the new mellotron. His work earned him the fans' nickname of 'the Sixth Moody'. He subsequently produced work by Clannad and Rick Wakeman, among others. He died in 2010.

An even more famous producer is Pete Waterman. He was born in Stoke Heath in 1947 and, educated at Whitley Abbey School, he left in 1962 with minimal skills to work for British Railways as a locomotive fireman at Wolverhampton Stafford Road engine shed. A love of railways has never left him, and he is now well known for his collection of heritage locomotives and his model railway. When the shed closed in 1963 he decided to pursue a career as a DJ, and was a regular at the Locarno ballroom in Coventry city centre for many years. He ultimately became one third of the hugely successful music production and song-writing partnership Stock Aitken Waterman, and the most successful producer-songwriter in British history. He received an honorary doctorate from Coventry University in 2001, and was awarded an OBE in 2005. Now in his seventies, he 'has no intention of slowing down', according to his website. 'His lust for life, excitement for new ideas and overall determination to continue making a positive change in everything he does burns as brightly today as it's ever done.'

Still in the world of music, singer Hazel O'Connor was born in Coventry in 1955, the daughter of a car factory worker. She attended Foxford School in Longford from 1965/66 until 1970, then ran away when she was sixteen and travelled around the world, discovering that her true love was music. She made her film debut in 1975, and is best known for the 1980 film *Breaking Glass*, for which she wrote and performed the soundtrack, to considerable acclaim. Coventry recognised her achievements with a plaque in the city's Wall of Fame in 2011.

On the stage, Ellen Terry was born into a family of actors in Market Street, Coventry, in 1847, and became one the most renowned English actresses of the late nineteenth and early twentieth centuries. She began performing as a child, and by the 1870s was being particularly acclaimed for her portrayal of Shakespearean characters. In 1878 she joined Henry Irving's company as his leading lady, and for twenty years was considered the leading Shakespearean and comic actress in Britain. She and Irving toured with great success at home as well as in America. She acted on stage until 1920, and even appeared in films from 1916 to 1922. After a career lasting nearly seven decades, she died in 1928, aged eighty-one. The Ellen Terry Building is part of Coventry University's Faculty of Arts and Humanities.

An earlier counterpart of hers was married at Holy Trinity church in 1773. Welsh-born Sarah Kemble married William Siddons, a young actor who had earlier joined the family's theatrical company from Birmingham. Sarah Siddons went on to become what many consider to be the greatest English tragic actress ever.

Eminent Coventry-born actress Ellen Terry is commemorated by this Grade II listed building in Jordan Well, part of Coventry University. Originally built in 1880, in 1931 it became the Gaumont Palace cinema, was acquired by the university in 1998 and given a major refurbishment in 2011.

Other actors born in Coventry are Nigel Hawthorn (1929–2011), unforgettable as Sir Humphrey Appleby in TV's *Yes Minister*; Charles Kay (b. 1930), seen in many TV dramas and a member of the Royal Shakespeare Company from 1963 to 1966; Billie Whitelaw (1932–2014), who, as well as many TV and film roles, worked in close collaboration with Irish playwright Samuel Beckett for twenty-five years and was regarded as one of the foremost interpreters of his work; Clive Owen (Keresley, b. 1964), film and TV actor since the late 1980s, who attended Binley Park Comprehensive School; and Chris Jury (b. 1956), best known for his role as Eric Catchpole in the BBC series *Lovejoy*.

Finally, in this 'whistle-stop' review of Coventry celebrities is Delia Derbyshire (1937–2001), the pioneering musician and composer who was born in Cedars Avenue, Coundon. She worked in the BBC Radiophonic Workshop in London, and is best known for her early electronic recording of the *Doctor Who* theme tune in 1963. There is a display dedicated to her, as well as the other Coventry-born musicians, at the Coventry Music Museum.

Coventry Today and Tomorrow

In 2011 Coventry had a population of 316,915, making it the ninth largest city in England and the eleventh largest in the UK. It is the second largest city in the West Midlands, after Birmingham.

Following the devastation of the Second World War, the city has pursued a continual programme of renewal and innovation. Tall and striking modern towers seem to be springing up everywhere, many for the increasing student population, and others for business occupation.

Many centuries of architecture jostle for prominence in the present-day Coventry city centre. This is the view across Broadgate and down the Precinct from the old cathedral tower.

The City Council has secured funding to invest in the city centre 'to ensure we create a legacy for local people after the city has welcomed the world for its year as City of Culture in 2021', retaining 'the best of the old alongside the best of the new'. Some £57 million has been invested in the city since 2011, with a further £10 million or so by 2021, resulting in significant private sector investment.

A recent development is the Phoenix Initiative, the most important regeneration project since the war, providing major environmental improvements for the benefit of not only residents and students, but also the huge numbers of tourists who visit the cathedral every year, encouraging them to stay longer and, of course, spend more! The intention is to create a new 'journey' through the city, both literally and metaphorically, extending and amplifying Coventry's standing as the city of international reconciliation. The development has now won a total of sixteen separate awards. It is intended to deepen Swanswell Pool and link it to the Canal Basin, creating an urban marina and a wide Parisian-style boulevard.

The River Sherbourne has been culverted beneath the city centre for many decades, and is now almost forgotten, but the plan is to reopen it, with a river walkway alongside it in parts of the city centre. Meanwhile, in 2012 the pedestrianisation of Broadgate was completed, providing a city centre venue for events such as fairgrounds and Christmas markets.

In 2017 the city was designated as the third UK City of Culture, in 2021. One initiative connected with this focuses on the cathedrals, old and new. The new cathedral is Coventry's best-known visitor attraction and provides the only large-scale indoor space in the city centre capable of seating in excess of 1,500 people for live performances. Meanwhile, the ruins will be developed to host a more diverse range of events. As the City of Culture Trust says, 'You can expect large-scale spectacle, music, dance, theatre and poetry as well as more intimate,

A hoarding outside the railway station makes it clear to arriving visitors that Coventry will be UK City of Culture in 2021, a proud achievement for the city.

celebratory cultural and heritage experiences in every ward of the city. We are also working with partners in Warwickshire, so expect that the impact will be felt within our neighbouring communities too.'

To emphasise this Coventry University says on its website, 'Coventry has a history of reinventing itself, Coventry is a city of peace, a city of innovation. From the Cathedral to the ring road, we have stories to tell and a quiet pride which can now shine! The jet engine, watchmaking, the Specials – so much has started here and ideas will continue to grow and develop.'

Today's Coventry is unrecognisable from the city that your author knew as a child in the 1960s, and one can be certain that it will continue to reinvent itself as future decades – centuries? – unfold.

Bibliography and Sources

Demidowicz, George, *A Guide to the Buildings of Coventry* (Tempus Publishing, 2003)

Fox, Levi, *Coventry's Heritage* (*Coventry Evening Telegraph*, 1957)

McGrory, David, *The Wharncliffe Companion to Coventry* (Wharncliffe [Pen & Sword], 2008)

Pickford, Chris and Pevsner, Nikolaus *The Buildings of England: Warwickshire* (Yale University Press, 2016)

Richardson, Kenneth, *Twentieth-Century Coventry* (City of Coventry, 1972)

Spence, Basil, *Phoenix at Coventry* (Geoffrey Bles, 1962)

Websites

www.britainexpress.com
www.britishlistedbuildings.co.uk
www.coventry.gov.uk
www.coventrysociety.org.uk
www.historiccoventry.co.uk

and the websites dedicated to the individual buildings, people and organisation, where appropriate.

About the Author

Although born in London, Will was brought up in Coventry, living there until he left to read English at Cambridge. He inherited from his late father, an enthusiastic amateur historian and archaeologist, a fascination with Coventry's history, and many of the books consulted for this work were part of his father's collection. Also, a distant cousin, William Frederick Taunton, published and illustrated an authoritative history of Coventry in 1870.

Today he lives in semi-retirement in Northamptonshire and divides his time between professional puzzle compiling and freelance book editing. A lifelong railway enthusiast, he has written several railway books, as well as some puzzle books.

He is married to Tricia, a retired professional librarian, and has two daughters, one a singer, the other a film producer.